FATHER LOVE

*Second Edition
Revised and Updated*

Praise and Testimonies for Father Love – Second Edition

There is only one perfect father. In Father Love, Eli Williams introduces us to our perfect Heavenly Father. Understanding God's lavish love toward us, his children, enables us to respond with a love like His toward our own children. As a father to four boys, pastor, and Biblical Counselor, I have seen firsthand the powerful influence that a father can have on his children. When a father seeks to honor God with his influence and responsibilities, there can be sweet, beautiful fruit that he and his children can enjoy as God empowers and blesses his efforts. The opposite is also true; when a father is self-centered, bitter circumstances surround him and his children, creating deep and long-lasting wounds. Human love is always responsive. We love God because God first loved us (1 John 4:10). Read Father Love today and begin to be amazed at God's faithful and persistent love for you.

- Sam Bryant
Pastor of Biblical Counseling
MABC from Faith Bible Seminary
Summit Point Church, Peoria, IL

Eli Williams' newly revised **Father Love** *is a spiritual and practical treasure chest filled with jewels of biblical guidance and support along with "golden" practical advice. The work is interspersed with beautiful and illuminating personal stories of healing, redemption, and deepening commitment for men facing real life challenges in their roles as both sons and fathers.*

Further, the book shares the structural framework for building a comprehensive church-based Fatherhood Ministry to address the national (and international) crisis of father absence in families and communities. This book shows us how we can save ourselves and save others from the personal, family and societal harms that emanate from the emotional and physical absence of fathers in our families and communities.

- Ted N. Strader
Ted N. Strader is an internationally recognized fatherhood expert and author of the Creating Lasting Family Connections Curriculum Series used in all 50 U.S.

states and several other countries. Ted's programs have published powerful results in peer-reviewed journals and have been recognized in several evidence-based and best practices listings. Among his many awards, Ted is a proud father and the recipient of the National Association of Marriage and Relationship Educators' Lifetime achievement award.

The first edition of Father Love inspired me to dedicate much of my time to fatherhood ministry. Eli Williams' profound insights into father absence and his biblical approach opened my eyes to the urgent need for men to embrace their God-given calling as fathers.

This new edition builds powerfully on that foundation while addressing a crucial gap in today's church landscape. Williams tackles the reality that no entity is better positioned to address the fatherhood crisis than the Christian Church. His new chapter, "What Christian Churches Can and Must Do," is a game-changer providing a comprehensive framework for church-based fatherhood ministry.

Williams makes a compelling case that churches have both a biblical mandate and unique opportunity to raise up godly fathers who serve as spiritual leaders in their homes and mentors in their communities. What sets this edition apart is his practical implementation approach—he doesn't just identify the problem but provides churches with a roadmap for developing sustainable fatherhood ministries that create "salt and light" fathers who impact their communities.

Every pastor, church leader, and father should read this book. Williams has given the Church both the theological foundation and practical tools needed to turn the hearts of fathers to their children and, in doing so, strengthen the very fabric of our society.

Bruce Stapleton
Author of Fathering Strong: God's Blueprint for Leading Your Family

FATHER LOVE

The Powerful Resource Every Child Needs

Second Edition
Revised and Updated

ELI WILLIAMS

FATHER LOVE
The Powerful Resource Every Child Needs

Second Edition
Revised and Update

Published by Movementum Press LLC
www.movementum.com

All rights reserved. No part of this book may be used or reproduced by any means, graphic, electronic, or mechanical, including photocopying, recording, taping, or by any information storage retrieval system without the written permission of the author except in the case of brief quotations embodied in critical articles and reviews.

This book is a work of non-fiction. Unless otherwise noted, the author and the publisher make no explicit guarantees as to the accuracy of the information in this book. In some cases, the names of people and places have been altered to protect privacy. Because of the dynamic nature of the Internet, any web addresses or links contained in this book may have changed since publication and may no longer be valid.

Scripture quotations taken from the New King James Version (NKJV), Copyright© 1982 by Thomas Nelson, Inc. Used by permission all rights reserved.

Scripture quotations taken from the King James Version (KJV) – public domain.

Scripture quotations taken from the Holy Bible, NEW INTERNATIONAL VERSION, NIV Copyright© 1973, 1978, 1984, 2011 by Biblica, Inc.
Used by permission. All rights reserved worldwide.

Scripture quotations taken from the New Living Translation (NLT), Copyright© 1996 and 2004 by Tyndale House Foundation. Used by permission. All rights reserved worldwide.

ISBN: 979-8-9985544-4-5 Hardback version

Copyright © 2016, 2025 Eli Williams

Table of Contents

About the Author ix
Dedication xi
Introduction xiii
CHAPTER 1 What is Missing? 1
CHAPTER 2 Father Love Defined 9
CHAPTER 3 Love is Patient and Kind 13
CHAPTER 4 My Father's Love 19
CHAPTER 5 My Awakening 23
CHAPTER 6 Love Does Not Envy 27
CHAPTER 7 Love Does Not Boast And Is Not Proud 29
CHAPTER 8 Fumbling the Fatherhood Football 33
CHAPTER 9 Love Is Not Rude or Self-Seeking 41
CHAPTER 10 For the Love of POPS 45
CHAPTER 11 Love is not Easily Angered 51
CHAPTER 12 Love Thinks No Evil 57
CHAPTER 13 Father, Father 65
CHAPTER 14 Love Finds Joy in the Truth 73
CHAPTER 15 Father Love is Nurturing 79
CHAPTER 16 Love Bears All Things 83
CHAPTER 17 Love Endures All Things and Never Fails 87

CHAPTER 18 Brad's Story of Father Love *93*

CHAPTER 19 Doing Battle for Fathers and Families *99*

CHAPTER 20 The Divine Armor *107*

CHAPTER 21 A Biblical Story of Father Love in Action *117*

CHAPTER 22 The Creator's Father Love *121*

CHAPTER 23 A Father's Spiritual Toolbox *135*

CHAPTER 24 My Dream *137*

CHAPTER 25 What You and Your Community Can Do *143*

CHAPTER 26 What Christian Churches Can and Must Do *153*

REFERENCES *163*

About the Author

Eli Williams is the Founder, President, and CEO of Urban Light Ministriesi, whose programs have included a suite of fatherhood programs that have impacted hundreds of low-income dads in six counties in west central Ohio since the late 1990s. He founded and provides visionary leadership for the annual FatherFest event, his community's annual celebration of fatherhood. The event, now a collaboration with the community's annual Juneteenth festival, includes ULM's Good Dad Awards, which honor men who are doing their best as fathers and father figures. Over the decades, Williams provided the vision for an award-winning community mobilization initiative called Fatherhood Clark County, which promoted healthy fathering county-wide, the Fatherhood Institute, and Urban Light's innovative Fathering Strong [ii] initiative.

Urban Light Ministries (formerly known as Lifeline Ministries) operated The Sonshine Clubs, which were weekly, after-school sessions that provided spiritual enrichment for more than 20,000 public elementary school students in Springfield, Ohio and the surrounding area from 1993 to 2020.

Williams has been married to Judith White-Williams since 1983. Together, they raised her biological son, Elijah, who was three years old when they were wed. Eli adopted Elijah when he was thirteen. Eli has an adult biological son, Joseph, and Judy has another son, Eric.

Eli's first career was as a professional singer and entertainer. As a teen, he co-founded and performed with The Four Corners, a Dayton, Ohio-based Motown-style quartet. He wrote three songs for the group, which he gave to them when he resigned in 1970 to pursue his calling to Christian service. One of the songs, "What Goes Around Comes Around," was later recorded by Michael Jackson and is on Jackson's 1972 *Ben*[iii] Soundtrack album, with songwriting credit attributed to the other former group members. He was the first to record Johnny Stephens (aka John Legend) when in 1993 he took the then 13-year-old phenom into the Dayton recording studio of his broadcasting college alma mater to co-lead a Gospel song Eli had written.

A now-retired professional broadcaster, Eli's personal ministry began in earnest in April of 1985 when he recommitted his life to Jesus Christ, quit his secular morning radio show on WCOM FM in Urbana, Ohio, and started a Sunday morning Christian music program. Over time, the show morphed into a weekly syndicated gospel music countdown called Hot Gospel 20 that was heard on traditional and Internet radio stations worldwide, until he retired the show in 2021.

Rev. Williams and his wife Judy partnered in a variety of independent outreach and church-based ministries over the years. To better meet the needs of people they ministered to through Urban Light, they planted Fountain of Life Church, and he served as Senior Pastor until the congregation merged with another church five years later. Currently, he is an Associate Pastor at New Hope Church[iv] in Springfield, Ohio, and often fills pulpits of various churches as called upon.

Dedication

Dedicated to my sons, all my spiritual sons, my grandson, Jorden Terrell Williams, and young men everywhere.

Introduction

This book is for men who are fathers, for those who aspire to fatherhood, and for those who support them.

Throughout this book, when I use the word "father," unless otherwise stated, I am including in the designation biological fathers, adoptive fathers, stepfathers, and other males who have an essential father-figure role in the life of a child.

I seek to answer the questions:

- What is Father Love?

- Does it really have value?

- How can I develop it for my children?

- Are fathers still crucial to children and communities?

- What distinguishes fatherhood from mere baby-making?

- What exactly is healthy, responsible fatherhood in the twenty-first century?

- What are the qualities and characteristics that make a man successful at fatherhood?

- What can I, my church, and my community do to promote and support healthy fathering for the sake of children and families?

This book aims to highlight the urgent need to re-establish healthy, committed, and loving fatherhood within our society for the well-being of children. While much has been written about the vital role mothers play, and rightly so, this work focuses specifically on fathers. It seeks to ignite a divine passion within fathers to love their children with the same boundless love our Heavenly Father shows us. My hope is that this heartfelt message serves as a powerful reminder to our culture of the immense value a father's love brings to children, families, and communities.

We will look at the cost of father absence to children, families, and society. We will contemplate the roots of father absence and the circumstances that contribute to it. I will share the hope I have found in biblical examples, my own father's story, and the real-life accounts of a few contemporary dads. I will share my dream of a better world through increasing the number of involved, committed, skilled fathers. We will also share our current efforts to support responsible fatherhood and healthy fathering practices.

If you are a father of minor children, I hope *Father Love* is an encouragement to you and that it strengthens your resolve to be the best dad you can be, despite the battles you may have to fight. I hope you will be inspired by the stories of real, fictional, historical, and biblical fathers cited herein. As we explore this topic, I aim to show that of all the characteristics, skills, and resources needed for healthy, successful fathering, love is the greatest of all.

I give honor to God, my Heavenly Father, for leading me in this endeavor. I am incredibly grateful to Kermit Rowe for his generous contribution of conducting interviews and for devoting many hours to editing the original manuscript, and to the invaluable contributions of Bruce Stapleton, who collaborates with me in many fatherhood-related endeavors for Christ. There are far too many others to name who have financially supported us, served on the ULM board, volunteered countless hours, and prayed for us and our mission. Thank you!

Last, but not least, I am deeply grateful to my wife, Judy, for her faithful support, often-thankless toil, and generous sacrifices as we serve together Our Lord Jesus Christ until He returns for us.

Some of the names of individuals in this book have been changed to protect their privacy.

All Scriptures are from the New King James Version, unless otherwise noted.

CHAPTER 1
What is Missing?

Beginning in 1993, my nonprofit organization, operated a weekly after-school children's ministry to hundreds of elementary school students in multiple locations called The Sonshine Clubs. After ten years or so, I began to wonder whether we were making enough of a difference in the lives of these precious kids.

Despite the best efforts of our dedicated volunteers and staff, and the heartfelt work of children and youth programs in my community, many of our kids were still experiencing negative outcomes. I came to realize that a large number of them live apart from their biological fathers.

Around that time, in a meeting of my county's Child and Family Collaborative, something profound occurred to me. As I listened to horror stories of abused, neglected, and traumatized children in our community, I asked questions. I learned that in each case discussed, there was a missing, unskilled, or irresponsible father or father-figure.

Aha! There it was! That revelation validated my suspicion that most social problems that negatively impact kids, families, and communities have their genesis in or are made worse by father absence. My subsequent study of the issues confirmed this as a fact. For this revision, I utilized Genesis AI to update the findings.

Here are samples of the compelling statistics:

1. **Poverty**
    - Children in father-absent homes continue to face significantly higher rates of poverty. As of more recent data, the disparity remains stark: children in single-mother households are substantially more likely to live in poverty compared to those in married-couple families. For example, recent analyses consistently show poverty rates for children in female-headed households without a spouse present to be several times higher than for children in married-couple families.[v]

2. **Drug and Alcohol Abuse**
    - The link between father absence and increased risk of substance abuse remains a critical concern. Research consistently indicates that adolescents from fatherless homes are at a dramatically greater risk of drug and alcohol abuse.[vi]
    - Studies continue to confirm a higher prevalence of drug use among children who do not reside with both their biological mother and father.[vii]

3. **Physical and Emotional Health**
    - The positive impact of a father or father figure on child well-being is continually affirmed by research. Studies consistently show that children living with married biological parents exhibit significantly fewer externalizing and internalizing

behavioral problems than children living with at least one non-biological parent. The stability and resources often associated with two-parent households contribute positively to children's mental and emotional health.[viii]

- The landscape of family structure in America continues to evolve. While specific numbers fluctuate, a huge portion of children in the U.S. still live apart from their biological fathers. Recent demographic data indicate that this impacts a substantial percentage of American children, with disparities persisting across racial and ethnic groups. For instance, the proportion of Black children living in father-absent homes remains notably higher compared to white and Hispanic children. This trend represents a profound shift from family structures observed in the mid-20th century.[ix]

- The societal cost of fatherlessness continues to be immense. While precise figures vary with methodology, the economic burden on federal and state governments assisting father-absent homes remains in the tens, if not hundreds, of billions of dollars annually. This underscores the substantial financial implications of father absence for public services and social welfare programs.[x]

The facts were undeniable. Yet, in 2006, no government agency, secular nonprofit, or Christian ministry in our community was making a sincere effort to address the father absence problem.

Chapter 1

After a few conversations with my friend, fellow minister, and social work expert Raymond E. Lloyd, Jr., I accepted this as a call to action. Urban Light Ministries launched its Fatherhood Program in October 2006.

Don't get me wrong. I have not been a perfect father—far from it. I have made my share of mistakes, any one of which could disqualify me from taking on a fatherhood mission. Yet, I felt compelled to do what I could to work toward addressing the father absence crisis for the sake of my community's children. How could we not, considering the plight of so many of our Sonshine Club kids.

I do not know any perfect dads. My own father was about as good as they came. But over the last few decades, I have discovered many things I wish I had known when raising my boys. Things my pops did not know or could not have done given his circumstances. I will share his story later.

As I investigated the father absence disaster, I came to two conclusions:

    A. Every child needs the unconditional love of a father.
    B. The absence of Father Love in the lives of children and neighborhoods is an American – and a worldwide crisis.

Is fatherhood a kind of panacea for all the social ills of the world? No, but it is an essential part of the solution. Here is why I'm persuaded of this. You've heard the story of the guy who was walking toward the riverbank when he saw a commotion. He became alarmed when he realized that there were babies in the river. Dozens of them! A crowd gathered, and people were frantically wading in to pull the babies out to safety. But they just kept coming. Someone yelled to him, "Hey, mister, don't just stand there, help us rescue these children. Can't you see they are in trouble?!" The man calmly answered, "You keep pulling them out. I am going upstream to stop whoever is throwing them in the river."

To our shame, we live in a society that throws babies into the river. We have stood by and watched and even facilitated the disintegration of family life. We know that the traditional family structure of father-mother-children is by far the best environment for children. Yet, instead of prioritizing the maintenance of that beautiful Creator-established order, we've diminished it as only one of many kinds of equal family structures.

We have allowed the development of poor communities to exist in the voids of once-great city cores, which are encircled by bastions of wealth. These high-density, low-income neighborhoods have fractured families, failing schools, high crime, boarded-up buildings, vacant lots, a lack of well-stocked grocery stores, drug trafficking, prostitution, gangbanging, drive-by shootings, and few well-paying jobs.

We shake our heads in disgust at the news reports of the horrible things that happen there. We reason within ourselves that it's the inner city, after all. What else can one expect?

Think, though, about the babies in the river. Consider the little children, the teens, the young adults who grow up in those environments who are receiving a clear message throughout their young lives: "I am worthless. No one cares enough to make sure I get a good education, that I eat well or that I am safe. There is no job or career for me. I do not have a future. Why shouldn't I get high, drop out of school, have sex, sell drugs, or rob a store? So, what if I go to prison or get killed? Who really cares? My own father does not even love me."

There are relatively few individuals who have what it takes to overcome those deplorable conditions to become successful in life. What about the others? Is it enough to work at helping kids beat the odds that they have been dealt by their circumstances — pulling them out of the river? Or should we not be working harder to change the odds, the conditions that are throwing them into the river? Isn't it past time for people of goodwill to ramp up serious efforts to go upstream?

This means improving schools and providing job training. It means supporting residents' efforts at cleaning up their neighborhoods and fighting crime. It requires encouraging investments in urban communities and providing good-paying jobs. It means strengthening families by promoting and supporting the formation of healthy two-parent households and facilitating the engagement of fathers in the raising of their children, whether or not they live with them.

It also means reforming systems, including government agencies and family court policies, which make it difficult for noncustodial parents to co-parent their children when the custodial parent is hostile. It should be considered a form of child abuse for a mother to deny her children the powerful resource of Father Love.

Last, but not least, what we need is a new movement of churches that are committed to developing fatherhood ministries within their churches to raise up men who are spiritual leaders of their families, servant-leaders in their congregations, and inspirational examples in their communities. To present my vision for what churches can do to answer this call, I have added Chapter 26 in this revision of *Father Love*.

The Emptiness and Pain of Father Absence—Phillip's Story

Raised by a single mom, Phillip does not remember ever having a father figure during his childhood. His biological dad abandoned the family, including three other siblings, before Phillip was born.

"I didn't really realize how that scarred me," said Phillip. That is, until he found himself in a cycle of bad relationships with women. "You are trying to fill that emptiness," he said. "You know your dad doesn't want you, so why would anyone else? That led to one bad relationship after another. You want to be wanted and needed."

Phillip finally found those desires filled with the birth of his own son, and has raised that son as a single dad. But he also found himself lacking in that role as well. "I didn't have a dad to show me how to be a dad," he said. However, there was one thing he did know. "I vowed that I would not do to him what was done to me," Phillip said.

In hindsight, Phillip realized this also reflected in his relationship with his Heavenly Father. "I only called on Him when I needed something," he said. "I thought I was saved, but I wasn't. When you don't have a father to rely on, you dot know how to call on the Heavenly Father."

After serving in the Army and a career in law enforcement, Phillip had an awakening in 2011—an experience many hurting fathers never have but is available to all. "I was searching for something to take away the pain and emptiness," he said. "I never knew what

Chapter 1

a real relationship was. I found out that you can't find that until you have a relationship with Christ. You can't truly love someone until you know how to love yourself."

Now Phillip, who was recently remarried, is hoping his son can find the same relationship with God that he did. "I think he sees the change in me," he said of his son. "The key is living that new relationship." And what about Phillip's father? "I hope that he found Christ, he said.

CHAPTER 2
Father Love Defined

What is Father Love? First, let us consider definitions of the word "love."

In the English language, "love" as a verb can mean tender affection for someone, desire for somebody, liking something very much, showing kindness to someone, or having sex with somebody.

As a noun, "love" can mean passionate attraction and desire, very strong affection, a romantic affair, somebody much loved, strong liking, something eliciting enthusiasm (such as sports or music), beloved, a term of friendly address, God's love for humanity, worship of God — even the score of zero in tennis.

Clearly then, we need to identify what we mean when we use the word in this context.

The Greek language tends to be more specific with words and their meanings. I have found it helpful to compare the four Koine Greek words that are translated "love" in the Bible to get a clearer understanding of the subject. They are:

- *Agápe*, which is supernatural love from God
- *Philia*, meaning friendship
- *Storge*, which is natural affection or family love
- *Éros*, which is sexual love

A father's storge love for his children should come naturally. It is instinctive. Even animals exhibit a kind of storge for their offspring. Having said that, storge love needs to be supported and nurtured in human males.

Chapter 2

Only humans, made in God's image, can possess Father Love at its highest potential. That's because it reflects the Creator's supernatural agape love for mankind. This super love, powered by the Holy Spirit, makes it possible for us to love as God loves.

It's so potent that it defies logic. Why would the Creator and Ruler of the Universe leave heaven in all its glory and perfection, take on the nature of human flesh in a sin-ridded material world and then die the worst of deaths to pay a sin debt that He didn't owe so we can go free? And how can He have such a strong desire for a personal relationship with his fallen children? The answer is He has a profound holy and powerful Father Love for you and me that love moves Him to action on our behalf.[xi] It is His very nature. He is love (John 4:8).

Agape is only possible for a human being when the Spirit of God produces it in the life of the Spirit-born believer. The New Testament writer Apostle Paul, in a Spirit-inspired letter to the believers in Galatia, explained that "fruit of the Spirit is love . . ."[xii] When agape love is generated in the spirit of a person, he is given the power to reflect God's loving ways in whose image he was made.

Father Love through the Lens of 1 Corinthians 13

In his God-breathed second letter to the believers in Corinth, Greece, Paul painted an enduring portrait of agape love.

> Though I speak with the tongues of men and of angels, but have not love, I have become sounding brass or a clanging cymbal. And though I have the gift of prophecy, and understand all mysteries and all knowledge, and though I have all faith, so that I could remove mountains, but have not love, I am nothing. And though I bestow all my goods to feed the poor, and though I give

my body to be burned, but have not love, it profits me nothing. Love suffers long and is kind; love does not envy; love does not parade itself, is not puffed up; does not behave rudely, does not seek its own, is not provoked, thinks no evil; does not rejoice in iniquity, but rejoices in the truth; bears all things, believes all things, hopes all things, endures all things. Love never fails. - 1 Cor. 13:1-8a

Verses 4-8 contain a list of sixteen characteristics of love. We will examine them in the following chapters with an eye toward understanding the power of Father Love.

Chapter 2

CHAPTER 3
Love is Patient and Kind

The first two characteristics found in 1 Corinthians 13:4-8 are foundational to the picture of love the Holy Spirit was painting through Paul, and to the formation of Father Love.

Love is Patient

First Corinthians 13:4 teaches us that love is long-suffering. That is, love is *patience on steroids*.

> *God, who is love, is patient with those whom He loves. He was patient with His rebellious people, Israel – often withholding judgment when they deserved it. In His love, He is patient with unbelievers, not wanting anyone to perish, but everyone to come to repentance. (2 Peter 2:9 NIV)*

Love is willing to suffer a long time under challenging circumstances. When a father has agape love, he can be more tolerant with the aggravations brought on by his children and their mother *without complaining*, even though it may involve torment for an extended period. Looooong suffering! It is only fair, since there is no doubt you supply plenty of annoyance for them, as well.

Patience is a part of Christian character. Like love, it is fruit of the Spirit. [xiii] When a person has God's Spirit dwelling in them, patience is supernaturally produced in their life. It is that calm and

Chapter 3

unruffled temperament with which the spiritually growing person can bear the evils of life, whether they proceed from persons or things. It is an enabling of the Holy Spirit!

Two-year-olds and teenagers will tax every ounce of Father Love within you. But remember, there is a kind of insanity that accompanies one during the passage through those developmental years. You were once there. So be patient with them!

Sometimes it is dealing with the children's mother that requires supernatural patience. Whether you are romantically involved with the mother or not, you must respect her for the sake of your children.

Someone has said the best thing a man can do for his children is to love their mother. To that, you may protest, "But you don't know that woman. She is a hater. There is no getting along with her!" To that I say, "Be patient with her. Ask God to help you love her the way He loves her, and you. Supernaturally."

Benjamin Franklin said, "If you would be loved, love and be lovable." [xiv] Remember, your children are watching. It's an opportunity to show them what Father Love looks like.

Love is Kind

What else does Father Love look like? Love is kind.

Kindness is defined as zeal towards another in a good sense, shown in doing mutual favors, benefits, and compassion for the afflicted. Notice that kindness is not just pity. Most people don't want pity. Kindness is *taking action on behalf of those who are suffering!* So, it requires a decision to act, to do something to help them.

In His kindness, God leads the unsaved toward repentance.[xv] This kindness, like the extraordinary patience described above, is fruit of the Spirit—supernaturally produced in the character of the Spirit-filled believer.[xvi]

Genuine Father Love enables one to be kind to others as well.[xvii] Harsh words, attitudes and behaviors are to be avoided.[xviii] This can sometimes be more difficult with those closest to us. Nevertheless, the Word of God instructs us husbands to love our wives and to not be bitter toward them. It also tells us to guard against irritating our children, which can discourage them.[xix] This can be difficult, but the Holy Spirit was given to empower us. As a Christian man takes the lead in his home, his wife and children tend to follow his example of kind-heartedness.

Non-custodial fathers are also wise to practice kindness toward the mother of his children, even though she may not reciprocate. That's another way the long-suffering nature of Father Love comes in. Who knows . . . her attitude may someday soften.

Chapter 3

A Cycle of Generational Fatherlessness Broken— Craig's Story

It's strange how the word "burden" can take on different meanings. Single father Craig was labeled as such throughout his childhood. "Never being told that he loved me, and that I was a burden, really hurt," said Craig. "I was missing that nurturing part."

Craig responded by making many bad choices as he got older, which led to drug addiction and broken relationships. It was not until he started working through his childhood pain that he gained perspective. "Once I got into recovery, I started seeing that my dad did the best he could," said Craig, adding that his dad was physically and mentally abused as a child. "His father did things to him that (my dad) didn't do to us."

Thus began the process of breaking his family's legacy of dysfunction, which Craig called "the cycle." Recovery was a constant battle, with as many setbacks as victories. That is, until his daughter was born. That was 10 years ago, and what many would see as burdens have become blessings.

"(She) was the motivational factor for me," said Craig. "With fatherhood, I have found that you are faced with demons and with God. One urges you to do bad and the other urges you to do good. You choose which one you'll listen to."

Craig chose God, got addiction help, enrolled in fatherhood training offered by Urban Light Ministries and set out to rebuild his broken life. "Being involved in a 12-step program and a fatherhood program makes you a better person, and so you become a better father," he said. "It transforms you into thinking like a father."

It also gave Craig the tools he needed to forgive his own father, and they now have a thriving, healthy relationship. Craig has the dad he always wanted, his dad truly knows who his son is and now has his grandchildren in his life, and the grandchildren have a grandpa who has learned how to properly love them and their daddy. Cycle broken — by God.

"I don't know why a lot of us hold on to resentment," said Craig. "We fail to accept what has happened and then we are separated because of that. It's just a lack of forgiveness. I found it with God, which allowed me to forgive my dad."

That doesn't mean there still aren't "burdens" in Craig's life. He has a toddler son who he raises alone. The child was born addicted to drugs and spent the first 64 days in a hospital's newborn ICU. His son's mother, also addicted to drugs, abandoned him as soon as he was born.

"What's so amazing is my life had already been set up so I could take care of my son," said Craig. That's because Craig had been there for his daughter, and he constantly battles the pain of vascular disease in his legs, which has left him unable to work. But is it a burden? Is his son? Is his daughter? Never! "What's strange is it has allowed me to be there for my kids," he said of his debilitating disease.

"Once you make that decision to get clean and stay clean, you kind of wake up to reality. I stopped running and took responsibility for my mistakes. And God has blessed me for it.

"I learned it is OK if you make new mistakes," he continued. "No one who raises kids does it perfectly. I learned that if you try and try and fall short, it's OK. And when you don't try, it's not OK."

Chapter 3

CHAPTER 4
My Father's Love

I was blessed to have a dad who modeled love. This is our story.

A young man's heart was broken into pieces as he watched his younger sister run down the country dirt road outside their humble Lowndes County, Alabama, home, sobbing, "Daddy, come back! Please don't leave us." That was many years ago, and that devastated young man was my father. That tragic scene could have been repeated generationally had my dad chosen the same path as his father. But he didn't, and it won't.

Young Ulysses Grant Williams, Sr. vowed that he would never, ever abandon his wife and children. With God as his strength and the church as his support system, my dad, the second oldest in his family, became a surrogate father to his siblings.

Ulysses was the son of Daniel, Jr. and Queenie Williams of Alabama. Daniel, Jr. left his wife—my grandmother, whom we knew as Mama Queen—with four children to raise on her own.

My mother's father left the same sad legacy. There was no Father Love in either of my grandparents' childhood homes.

Despite that awful experience, my father, whom they called Uly, came to faith in Jesus Christ as a teenager. The family's church recognized his maturity early and appointed him to the office of Junior Deacon.

Chapter 4

He married his high school sweetheart, Winnie Bowie, and worked the family farm until relocating his family to Dayton, Ohio, in 1954. He labored as a full-time city employee while also working part-time jobs to provide for his 13 children. He had an amazing Father Love and a strong work ethic.

Dad truly lived his faith in the way he loved and respected his wife and loved and cared for his children. Before he died of cancer in 1995, he provided a living example of Father Love for his children and all who knew him.

First, as a Christian, and second as an African American male, Dad was the kind of father that America has too few of today. His commitment to his family made him an asset to the whole community and to our country. Our family never spent a day on any form of public welfare. We never lived in a rented house.

Were we rich? Not at all. Indeed, we were considered poor by American standards. But we children didn't know it, because we had everything we needed. My father loved his Heavenly Father, he loved his wife, and he loved his children.

I don't recall him ever saying "I love you, son" with words, but he demonstrated it by keeping his commitments. His firm yet kind way of parenting endeared him to his children and gave us a mental model of Father Love. This powerful resource has blessed our family for generations.

Dad's decision to be a faithful Christian, loving husband, and committed father, despite the horrible example provided by his own father, reversed what could have been a curse on his family line. Thanks to his example, the nine Williams boys and the four Williams girls also became hardworking adults, with none going to prison.

We can only hope to be half the dad he was. It is for reasons like these that the Bible tells us to "Honor your father and mother (Eph. 6:2). My father, and millions like him, deserve recognition and celebration for the numerous ways in which they contribute to the well-being of children, families, and society. Oh, that every child could benefit from Father Love like I have!

Our dad led by example. As an illustration of the kindness he showed to others, I remember being a youngster and watching him go outside to offer a glass of cold water to a Caucasian workman who was laboring on our street in the hot sun. A man of peace, I never heard him, or my mother speak ill of other people, or blame his struggles on "the white man." He made a deep impression on me as he lived his faith every day by loving others. He never raised his voice at my mother or hurled profanity at her and never raised his hand to strike her. If they ever argued (of course, there must have been disagreements), they took it to the privacy of their bedroom and resolved it. Even if Facebook had existed back then, I seriously doubt either of them would have aired their conflicts for all to see.

It seemed he worked all the time. Yet, he was fully engaged in his church life as a senior deacon. When our black rotary phone would ring with a call about some need at the church, he would respond... sometimes to the understandable chagrin of our mother. But it was very rare that I would hear her complain.

Was Dad perfect? Of course, he wasn't. Still, he did an excellent job as a dad — one person with a lot of responsibilities. He never got to build a strong one-on-one relationship with me, because he just couldn't spread himself any thinner. We all understood that. But honestly, that doesn't mean there haven't been consequences for

Chapter 4

me or my siblings because of the lack of quantity and quality time with our daddy.

I didn't realize how much I had missed from not being with him more and developing a close personal bond until I was fifty-five years of age. It is essential to note how I came to realize that I had a father hunger.

CHAPTER 5
My Awakening

It was a Saturday morning in October of 2006. I was fifty-five years old at the time, we had just begun our Urban Light Ministries Fatherhood Program, and I was sitting in on a Nurturing Fathers class being facilitated for a handful of men by Raymond E. Lloyd, Jr., a pastor, expert in social work, and one of my personal mentors. Each participant was asked to take a few minutes to do some quiet, private introspection about their childhood. We were instructed to reflect privately on growing up, including what life was like as boys, the kind of relationships we had with our fathers, and what our dads were like.

As I let my mind travel back in time, the memories were mostly pleasant. I felt gratitude for my parents and a sense of having been blessed by God. Then it hit me. I didn't really know my father intimately. And he didn't really know me!

In that moment, a profound sadness came over me. A lump developed in my throat, and I felt like sobbing. I couldn't remember hugs and kisses. I could not recall my father ever being at my school events and performances. In that impactful moment, I didn't doubt for a nanosecond that Dad loved me—and I am incredibly grateful for that. It's just that there were so many experiences we hadn't shared, so many questions that I wished that I had asked him during the various stages of my life, so many things I regret not discussing with him, even as an adult son.

Chapter 5

That experience also made me come to grips with my failures as a parent. I had become like my father in many ways! Even though I didn't have thirteen children to co-raise on a common laborer's income, I had not developed a close personal bond with my boys. Intimacy with them had been sacrificed in deference to earning a living, building a career, serving the Lord, the church, and the community. Those are not bad things, but I had my priorities out of order and didn't realize it until they were fully grown.

I thought I had been a pretty good dad. Now I know better. It hurts to think about all the opportunities to spend time with my boys that I blew. Why do I dedicate myself to working with fathers? Because I see the urgent need to create spaces where men can openly share, be vulnerable, and connect authentically about their lives, their dreams, and their difficulties. My mission is to equip them with the insights to bypass the painful mistakes that I, my dad, and countless fathers like us have made in raising our children.

I had a good start with Joseph Eli, whom I nicknamed JoJo. Unfortunately, my nine-year marriage to his mother began to fall apart, and we divorced in 1980. I also renounced allegiance to the Jehovah's Witness organization to which our young family had been adherents. Because his mother was still under the control of the Watchtower Society, she complied with their ban on family relationships between Jehovah's Witnesses and former members. That was a devastating blow to my relationship with JoJo, who was nine years old at the time. Naturally, he didn't want to fall out of favor with his mother and all his Jehovah's Witness friends.

I fell in love with and married my current wife, Judy, in 1983. When JoJo was in high school, he came to live with me and my new family in Springfield, against the wishes of the Jehovah's

My Awakening

Witnesses. That was a joyous time for me, but a season of internal conflict for JoJo. I grew increasingly concerned about his psychological well-being. He would attend church, something strictly forbidden by the Watchtower Society, and even played in the church worship band. Then, when visiting with his mother, he would flip a switch and become a Jehovah's Witness again. This persisted for some time. I suggested that for his own mental, emotional, and spiritual health, he needed to make a choice. He chose to return to his mother. I totally understood the decision and respected him for it. Was that the right thing to do for his sake? I hope so.

My second son, born Alphonso Elijah Thornton, came into my life with my marriage to Judy. He was three years old at the time. When he turned thirteen, I was able to adopt him as my own. He chose to change his name to Elijah Lee Williams. Throughout school, Elijah was active in football, track, and other activities. Although I made the effort, attending all his events was difficult as I struggled to earn a living as a poorly paid small-town broadcaster and, later, a radio station account executive. That's not to mention the various side-hustles to earn money for the family. Being very active with church responsibilities and having accepted my calling to Christian ministry, I had a real juggling act on my hands.

I have since come to realize my mistakes in not balancing it all with a higher priority on family. Since a "do over" isn't possible, the least I can do is try to help young dads avoid making the same choices. My awakening also confirmed that I had been called by God to the mission of strengthening families by increasing the number of children with loving, committed, skilled, and present fathers. I want to see every child blessed by the powerful resource of fully developed and fully engaged Father Love.

Chapter 5

CHAPTER 6
Love Does Not Envy

Interestingly, the first two of the sixteen characteristics Paul listed in 1 Corinthians 13:4–8 are positive, but the third, envy, is not. It's as essential to know what love is <u>not</u>, as it is to know what love <u>is</u>. "*Love does not envy . . .*" (1 Cor. 13:4).

Envy is a painful or resentful awareness of an advantage enjoyed by another, joined with a desire to possess the same advantage. Why is it so bad, and why is it opposed to love? Consider this: How do you feel when someone you know receives a promotion, gets a new house, a new car, or is blessed with some spiritual gift? The sinful human tendency is that jealousy rises within, and we become resentful, or perhaps even angry. Love does not behave that way because love does not envy.

If the mother of your child has moved on romantically and has a new man who makes more money and can buy her and your child things that you can't, that's a difficult thing to swallow. Resist the prideful temptation to be envious. Have enough Father Love for your child that you can be grateful for the blessing they have received. It doesn't make you less of a man or father. You can still provide for your child what only you can give—your Father Love. Rather than envy, it is more loving to rejoice with those who rejoice.[xx]

Whereas love is fruit of the Spirit, envy is a work of the flesh—akin to sexual immorality, witchcraft, hatred, fits of rage, selfish ambition, and the like. The Word of God warns that those who practice such things "shall not inherit the kingdom of God (Gal. 5:19-21 KJV)." Envy is a serious matter. Don't be fooled into thinking that it causes no harm. Listen to what the Apostle James, under the inspiration of the Holy Spirit, warns us concerning envy:

> *But if you harbor bitter envy and selfish ambition in your hearts, do not boast about it or deny the truth. Such "wisdom" does not come down from heaven but is earthly, unspiritual, of the devil. For where you have envy and selfish ambition, there you find disorder and every evil practice. - James 3:14-16 NIV*

Much of the disorder in the world is caused by a lack of love. Envy and other sinful attitudes toward others cause discord, strife, friction, covetousness, and jealousy, which drive out love. It can easily lead to immoral behavior, including murder. The one who loves can suppress the tendency to be jealous or resentful when someone else is blessed. As fruit of the Spirit, love has power over envy, which is a work of the flesh—our evil inclinations. Here is what Apostle Paul writes, "I say then: Walk in the Spirit, and you shall not fulfill the lust of the flesh" (Gal. 5:16-17).

When Christians live in the Spirit, we won't surrender to our sinful leaning toward envy. The Holy Spirit gives us victory over the flesh, and love enables us to celebrate with those who celebrate. With this divine empowerment, Father Love leads us to a winsome personality that appeals to our children and others whom we impact.

Oh, how the world is hungry for Father Love! I wish I had come to understand its power much sooner in my life as a parent.

CHAPTER 7
Love Does Not Boast And Is Not Proud

The next two of the sixteen characteristics of love in 1 Corinthians 13, pride and boasting, are also negative. They may be socially acceptable to many today, but they are not pleasing to God. They are spiritual poison and are destructive to good human relations. They certainly aren't behaviors to model for children, and they are not loving.

First Corinthians 13:4 (NIV) informs us that "Love does not boast and is not proud."

To boast is to praise oneself, or to brag. Pride is thinking too highly of oneself. It is full of haughtiness and arrogance. These attitudes and behaviors are commonplace in contemporary society, just as the Bible predicted. Here is how 2 Timothy 3:1-2 reads:

> *But know this, that in the last days, perilous times will come: For men will be lovers of themselves, lovers of money, boasters, proud – having a form of godliness but denying its power. From such people, turn away!*

Self-pride, racial pride, cultural pride, athletic pride, gender pride, family pride, national pride, religious pride, church and denominational pride—they are not from the Father but are of the world. (1 John 2:16) According to Proverbs, known by many as the Book of Wisdom, a proud heart is sin (Proverbs 21:4) and pride goes before destruction (Proverbs 16:10). God resists the proud and gives grace to the humble (James 4:6).

Humility, the opposite of pride and boasting, is a mark of one who loves God more than himself and who loves others the way he loves himself. Love is the remedy for pride and boasting. Bible commentator Matthew Henry said: "Love subdues pride and vainglory." [xxi] In other words, a person who loves is not self-conceited and claims no honor, power, or respect that does not belong to him. He or she is not apt to despise others or trample on them with contempt or scorn. The person who loves is not bigoted, prejudicial or racist but thinks of others as equals. Those who have brotherly love will, in fact, go a step further. Paul admonished Roman believers to: "Be devoted to one another in brotherly love. Honor one another above yourselves (Rom. 12:10 NIV)."

To the Philippians, Paul advised:

> *Do nothing out of selfish ambition or vain conceit, but in humility consider others better than yourselves. Each of you should look not only to your own interests, but also to the interests of others. - Philippians 2:3–4 NIV*

If we don't want our children to be proud and boastful, we must not be that way ourselves. We must never forget that they are watching and learning from us. The way to be blessed is to turn from a prideful attitude. "Humble yourselves, therefore, under God's mighty hand, that he may lift you up in due time . . . (1 Pet. 5:6 NIV)."

The person who loves humbles himself, and God exalts him. In fewer words, "The way up is down." When all people who genuinely love God humbly seek His face for help in turning from wicked pride, God will forgive and heal us.[xxii] May men and fathers lead the way in humility.

A Family Transformed by Father Love—Mike's Story

Mike's first seven years were fatherless, and even when a stepfather did enter the picture, his home was still full of fighting and alcohol abuse. "When you don't have a dad in your life, you are kind of rudderless, especially when you are young," he said, looking back on his childhood.

"At first, you are rebelling. You are angry. I think you are crying out for attention. That's how I got attention anyway." However, it wasn't the kind of attention you'd want. When Mike was in the third grade, his mother was told by school officials that he was on a path that would end at the jailhouse.

So how did Mike go from a juvenile delinquent in training to becoming a powerful head of a county economic development organization? Something happened that turned everything around—his stepfather found God, and Mike found a father.

"As a young boy, you don't really understand that" said Mike of the impact that fatherlessness had. "You just want a father. Looking back on it, when my [step] dad became a Christian, things began to change in our house," he said. "And it seemed they changed overnight. It had a huge impact on my mom, then on me, and my brother and sister. It changed our lives forever." Indeed, Mike's stepfather eventually adopted him and his siblings.

"God has a way of letting us know that He is a father of the fatherless," he said. "A lot of times, we set our lives to be about money and power, but it is really about love and relationships." Granted, the initial adjustment was hard on Mike.

Chapter 7

"Dad was a disciplinarian; he believed in spanking," he said. "Looking back, that discipline changed my life. When you get older, you understand it more. I was very lucky." Indeed, many kids don't get a stepfather who changes their lives for eternity.

"I praise God for bringing a man into my life who was willing to be a father to me," Mike said. "I had what a lot of people have never had, a father experience that couldn't have been better."

Mike's stepdad passed away at the age of fifty, after a battle with prostate cancer. But what his father showed him about faith and love caused Mike to call on Jesus as his personal Savior. "He knows our hearts, and He wants to give us our deepest desires," he said. "God can change a life."

CHAPTER 8
Fumbling the Fatherhood Football

The game of football is rich with illustrations that can apply to fatherhood and father absence.

The goal of football is to get the ball into the end zone for a touchdown. But during the process, sometimes the ball carrier drops the ball. The dreaded fumble. It's mishandled during a hike, a hand-off, after a pass catch or during a punt or kickoff return. Sometimes the ball is punched out by a tackler.

How disheartening it is for the player, teammates, coaches, and fans when a fumble happens. Instead of being on offense and making moves toward the end zone, now suddenly they're on defense going the other way. When the opposing team scores because of a fumble, it is like having salt poured into an open wound. It can cost a team the game. Too many fumbles can cost a player his starting position and may even cost a coach his job. The object of fatherhood is to work as a team with the child's mother to get their offspring across the goal line of adulthood, safe, healthy, and contributing to society. Unfortunately, the fatherhood football is being dropped way too much.

The Causes of So Much Fatherhood Fumbling

Today, an ever-increasing number of children are being raised apart from their fathers. Approximately 18.3[xxiii] million children in the U.S. live in a home without a father figure (biological, step, or adoptive). This represents about 1 in 4 children. Some sources suggest a slightly higher figure, indicating nearly 24.7[xxiv] million children (33% of all children) live apart from their biological father.

Most often, father absence is caused by divorce and the separation of the parents. When parents separate, especially if the father moves out of the home, the level of direct involvement and financial support often decreases. Parental alienation, where one parent actively undermines the child's relationship with the other parent, can also contribute significantly.

Socioeconomic challenges such as poverty, unemployment, and lack of education are also drivers of father absence. Fathers facing economic hardship, unemployment, or limited job prospects may feel unable to adequately provide for their families. This can lead to disengagement or a sense of failure, sometimes resulting in their absence. Like unemployment, lower educational attainment can limit opportunities and contribute to financial instability, which in turn can impact a father's presence.

A significant and growing cause of father absence, particularly in certain communities is incarceration. Incarceration leads to physical separation, disrupts parent-child bonds, and often results in decreased financial resources for the family. The stigma associated with imprisonment can also make it difficult for fathers to maintain contact or for families to facilitate visits.

A substantial percentage of fumbles is caused by casual sexual activity, often between people who are not married to each other, resulting in children born to unwed mothers. In these situations, the father may not establish a stable co-parenting relationship or may not reside with the child from the outset. The instability of cohabiting relationships can also lead to father absence if the parents' relationship ends.

Sometimes, fumbling is because of personal and behavioral issues. Some fathers may simply not be willing to take on the responsibilities of parenthood, prioritizing personal lifestyle or other interests over their children's needs. Drug and alcohol abuse can severely impair a father's ability to be present and engaged in their children's lives. In cases of abuse or neglect, a father's absence may be necessary for the child's safety and well-being. Even when physically present, a father can be "absent" emotionally, failing to provide the necessary nurturing and support for their children's development.

Factors that are legal and societal in nature also contribute to father absence. For example, historically, custody laws have often favored mothers, potentially making it more challenging for fathers to maintain consistent involvement after separation. In addition, while evolving, traditional societal expectations about fatherhood (e.g., primarily as a breadwinner) can sometimes lead to fathers disengaging if they feel they are not fulfilling that role.

For others, it is generational. The factors cited often interact and can create a cycle of disadvantage. The absence of a father can, in turn, contribute to adverse outcomes for children, such as increased risk of poverty, academic difficulties, and behavioral problems, which can then perpetuate the cycle in future generations. Sometimes, it's as simple as people parenting the way they were parented.

Whatever the causes, the consequences of all this fatherhood fumbling for children, families, communities, and the nation are severe. President Obama put it this way in a speech delivered from the White House on Father's Day 2009:

> *In many ways, I came to understand the importance of fatherhood through its absence – both in my life and the lives of others. I came to understand that the hole a man leaves when he abandons his responsibility to his children is one that no government can fill. We can do everything possible to provide good jobs and good schools and safe streets for our kids, but it will never be enough to fully make up the difference. That is why we need fathers to step up, to realize that their job does not end at conception; that what makes you a man is not the ability to have a child but the courage to raise one.*[xxv]

Powerful words! But almost two decades later, the absence of fathers remains a crisis. Children in father-absent homes are still nearly four times more likely to be poor. Those words were said in 2009 and as of 2025, not enough has been done to change things. Frankly, as Obama said, it's more than a government can do.

Furthermore, there is not much support for the fathers who have tried to step up. Quite often, the opposite happens. Some noncustodial fathers are being opposed at nearly every turn by the mothers of their children, by some family courts, and by too many child support enforcement agencies. The separation of these two county government entities often works against these fathers by requiring child support payments but not enforcing those same fathers' parenting time rights. That's because child support orders are court-enforced, but parenting time rights often are not. This is truly an injustice. Change is happening in some states, but not fast enough. This breeds resentment, anger, and often withdrawal. The problem of father absence worsens as many fathers stop trying.

In the realm of fatherhood and family, a lot of fumbling is going on in the U.S. It is everywhere. With this crisis, as is the case with other social and economic disasters, the well-known adage rings true: "When America catches a cold, minority and poor communities get pneumonia."

Recovering the Fatherhood Football

Fortunately, a fumble need not mean the end of the football game. The fumbler has an opportunity to recover the ball if he reacts quickly, or one of his teammates can. There is hope! In my personal work with fathers since 2006, I have found that most men who live apart from their children want to be good fathers. They yearn to spend more time with their children and to be able to provide for them. I have also learned that many fathers who are physically present and desire to be the best parents they can be don't know where to turn for help or are hesitant to reach out.

As communities, we do ourselves a great favor by supporting fathers who have made genuine commitments to their children. Even those who have made bad choices in their past, are estranged from their children's mothers, are recovering from addictions or have been incarcerated can develop a strong Father Love. We should encourage and empower them to spend time with their kids. Custodial mothers and government systems should clear a pathway for them. Employers should do what they can to employ them.

Churches should provide a support network for fathers in their journey to sustainability. Those men need resources such as parenting and relationship education, job training, jobs, budgeting help, social services, legal assistance, coaching, and other resources to recover their roles as dads. This represents an excellent Christian

Chapter 8

ministry opportunity! This is a new focus of my work – helping congregations develop comprehensive church-based fatherhood ministries. I provide information about that at the end of this revision in the newly added Chapter 26.

As a society, not just fathers, we have indeed fumbled the fathering football. By not providing support to struggling fathers and offering disdain instead, we dishonor fatherhood and anger well-meaning, non-custodial fathers. Some get so frustrated that they give up trying.

Government efforts to help poor families have failed to consider the importance of low-income fathers in the lives of their children. As a response to the Great Depression of the 1930s, President Franklin Delano Roosevelt led the enactment of what became known as the New Deal, a series of welfare policies that provided work, jump-started economic recovery. He instituted welfare for the poor, elderly, and unemployed. One of the key provisions of the New Deal was a program known as Aid to Families with Dependent Children (AFDC), aimed at providing welfare for single-mother families.

"The implementation of means-tested welfare programs like food stamps, public housing, Medicaid, and day care during President Lyndon B. Johnson's 'War on Poverty' in the mid-1960s has been a subject of debate. It has been argued that certain design features of these programs indirectly incentivized single-parent households, leading to disproportionate negative consequences for the African American community's family structure." I believe these programs worked against the formation of two-parent families.

Before the Welfare Reform Act of 1996, a mother on welfare generally received roughly 10 to 20 percent more money from the government if she was single rather than married.[xxvi] All of this has been devastating to society, especially African American children, as the government replaced fathers and became a parenting partner with mothers of minor children. This proved to be a huge mistake. Simply stated, government is a pitiful parent because it cannot love. Government, however, is an essential partner in this.

What is it that fathers can contribute to their children's well-being that makes them indispensable parents, providers, and partners? Love! *Nothing* can replace the powerful resource of fully activated Father Love.

Make no mistake, it is not only low-income fathers who fumble the fathering football. Children of middle-income and wealthy dads are often deprived of a close, personal relationship with their dads as well. When the focus of our time and energies is on building careers and businesses, the children suffer. We may be able to give them more stuff, but what they want more of is us.

Remember, children spell love T-I-M-E. Kids say they'd rather have more time with their dad than more toys. Even altruistic activities such as community volunteer work and Christian missions, as vital as they are, do not deserve to be prioritized above a father's time with his children. Just as the time-tested saying goes, "Charity begins at home."

Dads know they need to be with their children more. In a recent Pew Research study, nearly half of all fathers (46 percent) said they spend too little time with their kids.[xxvii]

Fully developed Father Love has the power to draw the possessor of it off the golf course, from the club, out of the gym, off the race track, from the video game, away from overtime work, out of the casino, and away from the extra church meeting to his home to be

Chapter 8

with his kids. It is there that he becomes all the father that he was put on earth to be. That's the power of Father Love.

CHAPTER 9
Love Is Not Rude or Self-Seeking

The sixth and seventh of the sixteen love characteristics of 1 Corinthians 13 are also what love is not. However, these two have sadly become culturally acceptable, as our society continues to drift further away from the godly-fathering model.

Love is Not Rude

Father Love is an invaluable tool for modeling civil behavior for children. And that is more important today than ever before. Have you noticed how rude and crude people are today? What has happened to society that such awful behavior is tolerated, even glorified, by some?

Children and youth are mimicking the behavior they see on TikTok, television, movies, and video games. The vulgar lyrics of music in subgenres such as death metal, punk, drill, mafioso rap, and trap songs pollute the minds of youth. Podcasters and shock jocks will say anything they can get away with.

Public profanity, and a general lack of manners and common courtesy are prevalent among adults. We see this crude behavior from politicians, elected officials, and people at town halls. Incivility is now a strategy for gaining political power. But, that is not the way of love.

Chapter 9

First Corinthians 13:5 tells us, "Love does not behave rudely," or as the New International Version puts it, "Love is not rude (1 Cor. 13:5 NIV)." People who genuinely love God and neighbors are polite, courteous, and gentle in manner and behavior. The key to a less rude and crude world is love, because love is not disrespectful. Armed with Father Love, men can and should lead the way in civility.

God's Word instructs, ". . . be an example to the believers in word, in conduct, in love, in spirit, in faith, in purity (1 Tim. 4:12)." Christians are to behave radically different from the loud, rude, and crude worldly crowd as an example to fellow believers. Beyond that, our lives are to be a witness to unbelievers. Paul said, "Walk in wisdom toward those who are outside (Col. 4:5). Certainly, that rules out vulgar, discourteous, harsh, unseemly conduct. Love simply is not rude. It is the solution to a mean, uncivil, and crude world. If we want our children to be respectful, polite, and courteous in a bad-mannered and vulgar world, we must model that behavior in Father Love.

Love is Not Self-Seeking

Do you want your children to be unselfish? Teach them how to love.

In his classic Commentary on 1 Corinthians 13:5, Matthew Henry said the one who is practicing love of God and neighbor "does not inordinately desire nor seek his own praise, honor, profit or pleasure."[xxviii] Jesus is our perfect example in this. He came seeking our welfare, not His own. He came to serve, not to be served.[xxix]

> *Being in the form of God, (Jesus) did not consider it robbery to be equal with God, but made Himself of no reputation, taking the form of a bondservant, and coming in the likeness of men. And*

> *being found in appearance as a man, He humbled Himself and became obedient to the point of death, even the death of the cross. (Phil. 2:6–8)*

God IS love,[xxx] and He demonstrated that love is not self-seeking but seeks the benefit of others. Love is the more excellent way and is the cure for selfishness. Followers of Christ are to seek the ultimate benefit of others. Love never seeks its own advantage at the hurt of others. Conversely, the one who loves often neglects his own welfare for the sake of others.

Consider Jesus' parable of the Good Samaritan.[xxxi] In the story, he exemplifies selfless love by deliberately going out of his way, facing potential danger, forgoing his own comfort, and even expending his own money—all to assist a complete stranger, someone from a different culture and faith. This remarkable act vividly illustrates love made manifest.

Someone motivated by love does not use his influence in the home, community or church to a personal advantage. He will not advance, enrich, or gratify himself at the expense and damage of his family, the public, or the church because love is not self-seeking. Out of Father Love, he chooses to serve others first and himself last.

Keeper of the Castle

In 1972, the Four Tops recorded what would become a hit song that provided a social commentary on fatherhood. In the song "Keeper of the Castle," lyricists Dennis Lambert and Brian Potter admonished fathers to love their children enough to prioritize the care of their children. It communicates lyrically some of what it means to be a loving dad and a faithful husband.

Chapter 9

You're the keeper of the castle

So be a father to your children

The provider of all their daily needs

Like a sovereign lord protector

Be their destiny's director

And they'll do well to follow where you lead.

Oh, how that message is needed now, more than half a century later!

CHAPTER 10
For the Love of POPS

Every child needs the love of "pops." That is what my grown son, Elijah, and many kids today call their fathers or father-figures. If you have a child, there are things you need to know about your significant, God-given role in your child's life. To communicate this, years ago, I created the acronym "POPS," which stands for: protectors, order keepers, providers, and stabilizers.

So, what does the acronym POPS mean?

P = Protector

The Creator has placed within fathers the instinct to be their child's guardian. Every child needs the secure feeling that comes from knowing that their father loves them and is there to watch over and protect them. No child should live in fear in their own home. Yet too often, boys and girls witness family violence or themselves become victims of abuse at the hands of someone in their own home.

Often, the perpetrator is the boyfriend of the mother, the mother herself, or, shamefully, sometimes even the biological father. According to the U.S. Department of Health and Human Services, kids with live-at-home fathers are less likely to be abused.[xxxii]

The popular African proverb, "It takes a village to raise a child," assumes that the village includes fathers who fulfill their roles in

Chapter 10

the lives of the children. It is said that Masai warriors, for example, greet each other every day with the question, "How are the children?" They answer each other, "All the children are well."[xxxiii] Those mighty warriors understand that the well-being of the children indicates the truest measure of the health and security of their community. They know that their mission as protectors of the tribe is to defend the village from internal as well as external threats to the welfare of the children.

It is a father's responsibility to work with his child's mother to ensure the physical, emotional, psychological, and spiritual safety of their child. Even live-away dads have this duty. The dedicated father is most likely to fulfill this obligation when encouraged and enabled to be consistently present in his child's life.

Just being around makes a difference in the level of protection he can give his child. Neighborhoods are safer for children when fathers are present. It is believed by some that the chief predictor of crime in a neighborhood is the percentage of homes without fathers.[xxxiv] Out of Father Love, a POPS tries his best to be his kids' Protector.

O = Order Keeper

Both boys and girls need fathers who love them and are present and engaged in their lives. We all know how out of control things can get when the father is not available to provide firm, loving discipline. Just look at the conditions in homes, neighborhoods, and public schools where dads are absent.

Bob Simon of CBS News first reported in 1999 on young male elephants that were killing rhinos in South Africa's Pilanesberg Park. Because they had grown up with no adult male role models, the juvenile delinquents had no idea what appropriate behavior was. Raging testosterone drove them to violence. After rangers brought in big bull elephants, they began sparring with the young males. No more rhinos died.[xxxv]

Involved fathers seek to work together with the mothers of their children to create a healthy, structured, respectful environment for their children, and to maintain order in the home. When he lives away from them it is more difficult—perhaps impossible. But because he loves them, he does the best he can to be their Order Keeper.

P = Provider

The first thing that comes to mind when addressing the support of children is money. But financial support is not the only thing children need from their fathers. Committed dads cooperate with mothers by also providing emotional, psychological, spiritual, educational, recreational, social, and other vital resources for their children.

In addition to the assets mentioned above, the non-custodial parent—usually the father—is the connection to the child's other side of the family. Grandparents, uncles, aunts, and even cousins can be valuable resources for children as they grow up, and throughout their lives. These familial resources provide a sense of belonging, heritage, and cultural affinity. A person's life can be enriched by knowing who they are and where they came from. The love of one's father's family is priceless. It starts with Father Love.

Supporting children should include encouraging and empowering both parents to participate fully in the child's upbringing. Along with the collection of child support where appropriate, governments should enforce equal parenting time for both parents. Fathers and all non-custodial parents should be assisted in being full partners in their child's holistic well-being.

Some fathers face financial disadvantages, making it difficult for them to provide financially. Some of those very same fathers are among the most committed to the loving care of their children. This too is a provision, and it ought to be acknowledged and honored by society for the value that it brings to its children.

S = Stabilizer

Responsible fathers bring stability to the lives of their children by their consistent, loving presence.

Such children are less likely to have numerous changes of address. Single-parent homes headed by low-income women tend to experience frequent moves. Recurrent relocation is disruptive and causes stress for children. Having to leave their school, their friends, and the comfort of their home once or twice in a lifetime is upsetting enough. To have it happen time and again is often very traumatic for a child.

During a study by the Warwick Medical School at the University of Warwick in the United Kingdom, researchers discovered that frequent school moves during childhood may cause mental health issues in later years. They interviewed twelve-year-old students to find out whether they had experienced psychotic-like symptoms in the previous six months, such as hallucinations, delusions, and thought interference. Students who had changed schools three or more times during their childhood were found to be 60 percent more likely to display at least one of the symptoms.[xxxvi]

According to the American Psychological Association, "The more times people moved as children, the more likely they were to report lower life satisfaction and psychological well-being at the time they were surveyed, even when controlling for age, gender, and education level." The research also showed that those who moved frequently as children had fewer quality social relationships as adults.[xxxvii]

Single parents who change partners repeatedly, unwittingly add emotional trauma to their children's lives. Serial relationships have the effect of repeatedly subjecting children to the loss of significant father-figures.[xxxviii]

For many children, the addition of a stepparent to the household is a stressful change. And when remarriages end in divorce, children are exposed to yet more stressful transitions. An article titled "The Impact of Family Formation Change on the Cognitive, Social, and Emotional Well-Being of the Next Generation" by Paul R. Amato points out that some studies indicate that the number of transitions children experience while growing up (including multiple parental divorces, co-habitations, and remarriages) is a good predictor of their behavioral and emotional problems as adolescents and young adults.[xxxix] As soon as the child gets to know the new adult male father figure, he leaves. It's like going through the divorce of one's parents repeatedly.

When a child's father is consistently present in his child's life, he becomes a powerful stabilizing force for the child, even when multiple other men enter and leave the picture. The child knows that his father will always be there. That's what fathers are meant to be. Involved, loving, nurturing, protecting, and present fathers can make a massive difference in providing safety, stability, and security for children, whether or not they live in the same house with them.

Chapter 10

Father Love communicates to his child: "No matter what, I will always be here for you." The absence of POPS in the lives of children and neighborhoods is destroying our way of life. We are suffering from the lack of Father Love. We ignore this at our peril. Fatherlessness is one of the great evils of our time.

CHAPTER 11
Love is not Easily Angered

One of the destructive factors in family relations is anger, which is another example of the sixteen characteristics of love in 1 Corinthians 13 that show what love is not. Unresolved anger issues are responsible for many broken homes and injured children.

Love is the answer for a quick temper! It is the antidote for domestic violence, child abuse, road rage, and other fits of anger, because love is not easily angered (or provoked, as in the KJV). Put simply, love keeps its cool. Proverbs 14:17 tells us: "A quick-tempered man acts foolishly . . ."

I can attest to the truth that reacting quickly out of anger causes one to do and/or say things later regretted. He who holds his tongue is wise, according to Proverbs 10:19. Love enables one to control his tongue.

When one loves God and others, love sweetens and softens the mind and restrains the tongue. "A soft answer turns away wrath, but a harsh word stirs up anger." (Prov. 15:1)

We have the perfect example in Father God, who is Love. He is not quickly angered. Listen to Nehemiah 9:16 – 17:

> *But they, our forefathers, became arrogant and stiff-necked, and did not obey your commands. They refused to listen and failed*

> to remember the miracles you performed among them. They became stiff-necked and, in their rebellion, appointed a leader in order to return to their slavery. But you are a forgiving God, gracious and compassionate, slow to anger and abounding in love. Therefore, you did not desert them.

What a wonderful example of long-suffering, grace and mercy. Jehovah God had every right to burn in anger and to exact harsh punishment for His ancient chosen people's disobedience. He chose not to.

His extravagant love perfectly balances His divine justice. Let us emulate Him in our dealings with our children, their mothers, and all others.

The Cure for Family Violence

Experts agree that family violence is a widespread problem. However, its actual magnitude is difficult to measure. The contributing causes of family violence are many, but the Word of God gives the key to a peaceful marriage relationship—love. Colossians 3:19 says, "Husbands, love your wives and do not be bitter toward them." Love is the solution, because love is not easily angered.

Ephesians 4:26-27 says to husbands, "Be angry, and do not sin. Do not let the sun go down on your wrath, nor give place to the devil."

God is quick to forgive and slow to anger. In love, *we* are to be patient with and kind to our children and spouses. And *we* are to quickly forgive, because love is not easily angered. Doing so makes it impossible for the devil to find a foothold in our relationship. Fits of rage, discord, and hatred are works of the flesh (see Gal. 5:19-21). If you are having trouble in this area, it may indicate a severe spiritual deficit in your life. If you tend to be angry with your spouse, or the mother of your children, or others in your family, get help right away.

Ephesians 4:30–32, in no uncertain terms, tells Christians,

> *And do not grieve the Holy Spirit of God, by whom you were sealed for the day of redemption. Let all bitterness, wrath, anger, clamor, and evil speaking be put away from you, with all malice. And be kind to one another, tenderhearted, forgiving one another, just as God in Christ forgave you.*

Pray that God, through the Holy Spirit, fills your heart with genuine love for your mate or the mother of your child. For love is patient, kind, and is not easily angered.

First Corinthians 13:4 - 8 makes it plain that agape love holds the key to better relationships. Since love "is not provoked" and "is not easily angered," it is the cure for family violence. In fact, loving your neighbor **prevents** violence toward everyone.

God has commanded Christians to love our neighbors as ourselves. The indwelling Spirit of God, who is love, produces gentleness and self-control in us. By walking in the Spirit, we can resist the temptation to react to offenses with violent words or deeds. Love is the solution, because love is not easily provoked.

Love has a superior way of responding to offenses

Jesus told His disciples in Matthew 5:9–12, "Blessed are the peacemakers, for they will be called sons of God." The more excellent way of responding to offenses is with love. Because agape love is not easily angered, one who loves answers unkindness with fruit of the Spirit. "But the fruit of the Spirit is love, joy, peace,

Chapter 11

patience, kindness, goodness, faithfulness, gentleness and self-control (Gal. 5:22-23 NIV)."

Because love makes us peacemakers[xl], it empowers us to love our families and neighbors. As a benefit, our own happiness is enhanced. Can love help one deal with those who hate him? Perhaps it is your baby's mother who is angry and unforgiving, although you are simply trying to be a better parent. Love is the believer's solution even when his enemy is harassing him.

Here are Jesus's words on the matter:

> *Blessed are those who are persecuted because of righteousness, for theirs is the kingdom of heaven. Blessed are you when people insult you, persecute you, and falsely say all kinds of evil against you because of me. Rejoice and be glad, because great is your reward in heaven, for in the same way they persecuted the prophets who were before you. - Matt. 5:10-12 NIV*

Love even enables one to rejoice amid persecution. That defies logic, but love is the more excellent way.[xli] Here is how the Apostle Paul instructs us to respond to evil:

> *Do not repay anyone evil for evil. Be careful to do what is right in the eyes of everybody. If it is possible, as far as it depends on you, live at peace with everyone. Do not take revenge, my friends, but leave room for God's wrath, for it is written: "It is mine to avenge; I will repay," says the Lord. On the contrary: If your enemy is hungry, feed him; if he is thirsty, give him something to drink. In doing this, you will heap burning coals on his head. Do not be overcome by evil, but overcome evil with good." - Rom. 12:17-21 NIV*

Love is not easily angered, even by one's enemy. By the power of

God's love working within us, we are to do good to them, even those who despitefully mistreat us. No one is worthy of this kind of consideration. But just as God in His great grace bestows His love upon us though undeserving of it, we are required by Him to love others.

The Rev. Dr. Martin Luther King, Jr. said, "Agape is disinterested love . . . Agape does not discriminate between worthy and unworthy people, or any qualities people possess. It begins by loving others for their sakes."[xlii]

Chapter 11

CHAPTER 12
Love Thinks No Evil

The last of the "love is not" statements is possibly the most powerful: "Love thinketh no evil." That's how the King James Version renders 1 Corinthians 13:5.

What does that mean for fathers, and how can it help us today when evil is all around us? The Living Bible puts it this way: "It [love] does not hold grudges and will hardly even notice when others do it wrong." The NIV renders 1 Corinthians 13:5 like this: ". . . it [love] keeps no record of wrongs." In plain language, when one has true love, he or she is quick to forgive and doesn't dwell on past offenses.

Sure, someone will say: "Hold on a minute! You're going to just let people get away with messing over you. You can't do that, or you're setting yourself up for abuse." For an answer, listen to the wisdom of Proverbs 17:9 (NIV) when it says, "Whoever would foster love covers over an offense, but whoever repeats the matter separates close friends."

The New Living Translation, Second Edition, makes it even clearer: "Love prospers when a fault is forgiven, but dwelling on it separates close friends." And these are the words of Jesus: "For if you forgive men when they sin against you, your heavenly Father will also forgive you. But if you do not forgive men their sins, your Father will not forgive your sins (Matt. 6:14-15 NIV)." Also: ". . . if you have anything against anyone, forgive him (Mark 11:25)."

Chapter 12

Yes, genuine love is quick to forgive and holds no grudges. It is the more excellent way and is a key to building great relationships. Because agape love thinks no evil and keeps no record of wrongs, one who practices it can overlook minor faults and offenses of others. Jesus asked: "Why do you look at the speck of sawdust in your brother's eye and pay no attention to the plank in your own eye (Matt. 7:3 NIV)?" By not sweating the small stuff, we "promote love," as Proverbs 17:9 suggests. After all, we've each got our own imperfections and personality quirks. It is better to ignore them in others. That's the manner of agape love.

Agape love is not inclined toward revenge.

Because love thinks no evil by keeping no record of wrongs, it is not inclined to seek revenge. Instead of getting even with someone, here is what the Apostle Peter tells us to do in 1 Peter 4:8: "Above all, love each other deeply, because love covers over a multitude of sins." Rather than looking for payback, the person who practices true agape love is eager to forgive.

In marriage, the offended mate does not give silent treatment or withhold sexual intimacy but seeks reconciliation before the sun goes down.[xliii] This is good practice in all relationships. Address offenses as soon as possible. Avoid phrases like "you always do that" or "you never do this or that." Name-calling is also out of bounds. Be respectful, brief, and specific. In very few words, communicate what the offense was, how it made you feel, and identify precisely when it occurred.

Be quick to forgive. That does not mean being quick to forget. Whereas God can forget our sins, we humans don't have that supernatural ability. We remember the hurts, disappointments, and betrayals. It takes time to forget. For deep wounds, it may take a long time. For us, forgiveness is a process. We must continue to forgive each other every time we remember the offense and feel the hurt. Perhaps this is why Jesus, when questioned by one of His disciples about forgiveness, answered the way He did:

> *Then Peter came to Him and said, "Lord, how often shall my brother sin against me, and I forgive him? Up to seven times?" Jesus said to him, "I do not say to you, up to seven times, but up to seventy times seven." - Matt. 18:21-22*

Seventy times seven is the biblical symbol for infinity. So, our Lord says, as Christians who have been forgiven, we are to forgive an infinite number of times—freeing the offending person from paying a price for the offense every time we remember it. When we no longer feel the pain of the offense, the forgiveness process is complete.

The one who is offended benefits the most from forgiveness. No longer feeling the pain means the wound has healed. Failing to forgive prolongs the suffering and can result in the development of a root of bitterness that sends poison throughout the body, soul, spirit, and mind. Forgive, and set yourself free. For more on forgiveness, I recommend the book Total Forgiveness by R.T. Kendall.[xliv]

Love does not seek revenge by telling others about an offense— thus harming the other's reputation. Remember Proverbs 17:9, "He who covers over an offense promotes love, but whoever repeats the matter separates close friends."

Love is not apt to be suspicious or jealous

Love does not suspect evil of another. When there is no solid evidence, love does not charge guilt upon another. And love doesn't go around digging for the faults in others but covers over and minimizes minor faults and offenses. Remember, "And above all things have fervent love for one another, for 'love will cover a multitude of sins'(1 Pet. 4:8)."

Love can change the world by making this a kinder place, but it must start with those who serve the God who is love. Children need to be surrounded by adults who practice these attributes of love. Father Love is powerful enough to lead the way.

Have you ever had someone tell you something unflattering about another? Did it cause you to see that person with a jaundiced eye afterward? Love will not easily give way to a bad opinion of another because "love thinks no evil." Love is apt to believe well of others. It tends to give others the benefit of the doubt. Agape puts the most optimistic face it can on circumstances that don't look good on the surface — hoping for the best for a person.

Almighty God gave us the perfect example of love when, as Romans 5:8 says, ". . . while we were still sinners, Christ died for us." Our charge is found in 1 John 4:11 (NIV): "Dear friends, since God so loved us, we also ought to love one another."

Faults and all, we must love each other. It is the most powerful resource in existence for building and maintaining healthy relationships.

But what if it's true? Love thinks no evil of another, but how does love behave when the evidence is clear that the negative thing you've heard about another is factual? Love still thinks no evil and will yield to a bad opinion of another only with regret and reluctance. Because love is always looking for the best in others, it will believe the worst about someone only when the evidence cannot be resisted. That is not naiveté, it is agape. And love is the more excellent way.

> *For when we were still without strength, in due time Christ died for the ungodly. For scarcely for a righteous man will one die; yet perhaps for a good man someone would even dare to die. But God demonstrates His own love toward us, in that while we were still sinners, Christ died for us. - Rom. 5:6-8*

In His great love for you and me, God sent His only begotten Son into the world to redeem us from the curse. He has commanded Christians everywhere to love each other and to love our neighbors. One of the ways we obey that mandate is by keeping no record of wrongs against us, and by thinking no evil of one another.

Love Does Not Delight in Evil

It is certainly not news to you that some of today's most popular TV shows and movies are filled with depravity. As I mentioned in Chapter 9 – Love is not Rude, some of today's popular music is laced with profanity. Video games feature gratuitous violence. If you remove the immorality, death, destruction, crime, vice, and corruption from today's entertainment, there isn't much left. That is simply unbiblical: "Love does not delight in evil (1 Cor. 13:6 NIV)."

When one possesses true agape love, one takes no pleasure in the suffering of others. Although much of what is depicted is fiction, a steady consumption of evil images desensitizes one to real suffering, making it less likely that one will show compassion. Parents must regulate what children consume.

Even nonfictional accounts of violence to others — such as the 9/11

Chapter 12

terrorist attacks, or the January 6 insurrection at the Capitol—when watched repeatedly may reduce our sensitivity to the suffering of the victims. We tend to become numb to the very genuine horror that thousands of victims faced that day. That's reason enough to limit our own and our children's exposure to images of violence—fact or fiction.

Love rejoices not in immorality. So then, is it an act of love to make heroes for entertainment purposes out of those who do injury to others? That would be contrary to love, wouldn't it?

Some of today's most popular actors have very few speaking lines, but if they can shoot, kick, or slice and dice other human beings, they are assured of millions of dollars at the box office. Sure, you can say that it's only make-believe. But wouldn't it be hypocritical for one who claims to love God to be entertaining himself with the very things God hates?

We should choose carefully what we watch because love "rejoiceth not in iniquity (1 Cor. 13:6 KJV)." The practitioner of God's love is not entertained by the depiction of demons, witches, warlocks, wizards, vampires, or other evil persons. Some shows even go so far as to portray these in a good light, making them heroes. The Bible asks: "For what do righteousness and wickedness have in common? Or what fellowship can light have with darkness? (2 Cor. 6:14-15 NIV)."

The person filled with God's love takes no delight in the works of darkness—even if they are a work of fiction. When one recognizes these for what they are—attempts to trivialize evil—it is easier to reject them as tricks of the enemy. Let us guide our children with Father Love by protecting them from such evil.

Love does not laugh at the misfortunes of others because "love does not delight in evil." Agape is simply not entertained by the jokes of comedians when the humor comes at the expense of someone's hurt or misfortune. Romans 12:15 tells us to "Rejoice with those who rejoice" and to "mourn with those who mourn." That's the way of love. Children learn from us what is funny. In love, let us teach them how to have fun without delighting in the hardship of others.

Since love does not delight in iniquity, should a loving person play practical jokes or lie to get a laugh? When one loves his neighbor as himself, he doesn't play jokes that may hurt others. Furthermore, because love "rejoiceth not in iniquity," the true lover of God does not tell jokes that involve lying to get a laugh and doesn't resort to vulgarity in an attempt to be funny.

Am I asserting that love is not fun? No. Proverbs 17:22 says, "A merry heart does good, like medicine, but a broken spirit dries the bones." The Lord wants us to have joy. So, enjoy life—laugh and have fun. There are many ways to find amusement without violating love. "Clean Comedy" is growing very popular today, proving that comedy need not be ungodly.

Love is not entertained by music that glorifies rape, suicide, drug abuse, drunkenness, greed, materialism, witchcraft, hate, sex, or violence. When I was a teenager, some of the music I listened to featured promiscuousness, drug use, and had anti-war protest themes. But now, as a Christ-follower, Gospel and Christian are my preferred genres. I occasionally enjoy smooth jazz, old school R&B and 80s Light Rock. I try to be quick to skip songs that Jesus would not enjoy listening to if he were in the car with me. Discernment is the key.

As parents, we must introduce our children and grandchildren to

Chapter 12

Christian music and other wholesome entertainment that suits their taste. Clean music in every genre, from hip hop to hard rock, is available. In this way, we teach them that love finds its delight in music that praises God, not in iniquity.

Love finds no pleasure in the things that God hates. The Bible lists three of them in 1 John 2:16 (KJV) when it says, "For all that is in the world, the lust of the flesh, and the lust of the eyes, and the pride of life, is not of the Father, but is of the world."

These lusts include sexual immorality, witchcraft, hatred, discord, jealousy, fits of rage, selfish ambition, disputes, conspiracies, envy, drunkenness, orgies, and the like. So much of the world's entertainment is filled with these things. We must make our amusement choices prayerfully so that our enjoyment is consistent with love.

How inconsistent, and indeed hypocritical, is it for those who are children of the God of Love to be amusing ourselves with the very things that He condemns? People of genuine love do not find pleasure in the iniquity of others — real or make believe — because "love does not delight in evil."

Help your children learn to be discerning when it comes to entertainment. If a father is not present and actively engaged in every aspect of his child's life, how can he be a resource for him or her when they make their entertainment choices? This is one of the great tragedies of our present world and represents a grave injustice to children.

CHAPTER 13
Father, Father

At around 3:30 in the morning of Oct. 30, 2009, I woke up from sleep with these words in my head. They were to the tune of the 1971 Marvin Gaye song "What's Going On."

There's too many of us missing
Children really need us
Loving, helping, hugging, kissing
You know we've got to find away
To stabilize the family here today

Little girls need you to stay
Boys need a hero
Who cares enough to show the right way
You know you want to find a way
To bring some loving everyday

Skipping out, missing out
Don't take a leave from your family
Talk to me so we can see

Chapter 13

What Is Going On?

America has a deepening quagmire. No, not the Vietnam War that Marvin Gaye lamented. We are fighting a global war against terrorists who are determined to destroy us and our way of life. As I write this, there are several conflicts that the U.S. is at risk of being drawn into. However, I speak of another crisis that is also putting our society at serious risk.

It is children growing up without men whose hearts are filled with Father Love for them and with a determination to be their children's protectors, order keepers, providers, and stabilizers.

Using my new lyrics to that great tune, here are more facts about this disaster:

"There's too many of us missing."

A vast body of social science research consistently supports the idea that, on average, a stable family with two married parents (a mother and a father) provides the most beneficial environment for children's well-being. This is often referred to as the "two-parent privilege" in academic discourse. The data indicates that a stable, two-parent, married household provides a framework that, on average, optimizes the conditions for a child's well-being and future success. Considering that, clearly, the crisis for children and society is real.

Children in Single-Parent Households

In 2023, approximately **25%** of children in the U.S. lived in a single-parent household, which is a slight decrease from the 27% reported in 2016. The majority of these households, about 85%, are headed by single mothers.

Father-Absent Homes

As of 2023, about **17.8 million children**, or around **24%** of children under 18, lived in a home without a biological, step, or adoptive father. While data on how many of these children have not seen their father in the past year or have never been to their father's home is not consistently tracked by major reporting agencies, the overall trend of children living without a father remains a significant social issue.

Children in Intact Families

Based on recent U.S. Census Bureau data, the percentage of children who grow up with married biological parents for their entire childhood has slightly improved. While it was about 50% in the mid-2010s, a 2023 analysis found that approximately **54%** of American children will spend their entire childhood in an intact family. Still a crisis. Contrast today's 54% to the post-war era, when about 80% of children could expect to grow up with two biological parents who were married to each other.

"Don't take a leave from your family."

The horrible legacy of slavery, the industrial revolution, women's liberation, the rejection of traditional values, unintended consequences of government programs and policies, a growing permanent economic underclass, and a plethora of other societal developments have conspired together to bring about the crisis of fatherlessness.

Chapter 13

Divorce, military deployment, gatekeeping motherhood, addiction, homicide, unwed parenting, and incarceration all contribute to the removal of fathers from children's lives. Not to be left out is the syndrome of stunted male development. What I mean by that is that it is taking much longer for boys to become mature and responsible men. Some never make it. A sure indication of immaturity is not taking responsibility for themselves and their children.

All the above, combined with a popular culture that celebrates misogyny, the thug lifestyle, materialism, and plain old selfishness, gives legitimacy to unwed sex and uncommitted parenthood. Having said that, the book *Doing the Best I Can: Fatherhood in the Inner City* by Katherine Edin and Timothy J. Nelson [xlv] sheds light on the fact that many men raised in the culture described above do take responsibility for their children and try to be good fathers. I've seen that in my work with fathers.

Such a determined Father Love desperately needs to be nurtured in men and supported so that fewer decide to leave their children for their children's mothers to rear alone.

"Children really need us."

Children do much better on just about every measure when they have a loving, committed, engaged, skilled father in their lives.

Those who live apart from their biological fathers are, on average, at least two to three times more likely to use drugs, to experience educational, health, emotional and behavioral problems, to be victims of child abuse, to become teen parents and to engage in criminal behavior than their peers who live with married (biological or adoptive) parents. [xlvi]

It was with good reason that the Creator made it so that contributions from both a male and a female are required to procreate. He had a great purpose in mind when He established that the man and woman were to be joined together as husband and wife for life, so that the next generation benefits from having two parents who love each other and are committed to caring for their children in a loving, safe, nurturing home. The further we get away from that ideal, the worse our society becomes.

Even when—for whatever reason—this arrangement doesn't work out between the two parents, their children still need both of their parents in their lives as parenting partners. Children need both their mothers and their fathers!

Children so desperately need Father Love that they will have a deep void in their inner being without it. They will spend a lifetime trying to fill that empty space, often with disastrous results.

Perhaps you know firsthand that hurt. Only the Heavenly Father Himself, whom Scripture calls "a father of the fatherless,"[xlvii] can fill that emptiness. If you are among the millions who are hurting because of fatherlessness, turn to the Heavenly Father. He *will* heal your wounds!

"Loving, helping, hugging, kissing."

Every child needs daily attention and affection from their moms and pops. When their parents fill that need, children are less likely to seek kindness and warmth from the wrong sources.

Love expressed in physical and non-physical ways from both mother and father is essential to the healthy development of children. Both boys and girls thrive when nurtured by their fathers. Fathers are instructed by Paul in the Holy Scriptures to "provoke not your children to wrath: but bring them up in the nurture and admonition of the Lord."xlviii

"Little girls need you to stay."

Father, your daughter needs you to be the first male to show her what it means to be unconditionally loved. To experience what it's like to have a man who tells her she is the most beautiful girl in the whole world. She needs a father who is a protector and a provider. A father who, together with her mother, brings order and stability to her life. She will likely not settle for any less of a man for a mate.

"Boys need a hero who cares enough to show the right way."

Boys need fatherly attention, discipline, and affection. They need a POPS that is present and engaged. They need someone who is a model of mature and responsible manhood. That kind of man demonstrates for his son how to honor females and how to love a wife. Kids seek and need the attention, approval, and adoration of their parents. They are at very early ages parent-pleasers. That's why sporting events, recitals, and artistic performances mean so much to children when the parents are there to witness them.

When Dad isn't there, children will seek male affection anywhere they might find it. But alas, what many will attract is the attention of sexual predators, drug dealers, gang leaders and others who lack Father Love and don't mean them well.

"Find a way to bring some loving every day."

Ninety-one percent of fathers and 93 percent of mothers agree that there is a father-absence crisis in America.[xlix] For the sake of children and the very future of our society, we must find a way of reversing this awful situation.

We fathers must turn our hearts toward our children even though we may live away from them. We can still communicate regularly. It makes a difference for them to know that their father loves them and cares enough to make the effort to stay in touch.

Incarcerated fathers can also have a powerful impact on their children. Their contact makes a difference for the kids. When there is no regular contact, the pain it causes their children can be unbearable.

Perhaps you've heard the haunting poem "Knock Knock"[1] by Daniel Beaty, the African American author and spoken-word artist, as he laments the absence of his imprisoned father. It says in part:

> *Papa, come home, 'cause I miss you.*
> *I miss you waking me up in the morning and telling me you love me.*
> *Papa, come home, 'cause there's things I don't know,*
> *And I thought maybe you could teach me*

Reach out to your children, wherever you are. Assure them of your love.

Chapter 13

Residential fathers must reorder their lives to make their children a higher priority than their own needs, careers, sports, and all forms of entertainment.

The lack of determined Father Love that does whatever it takes, no matter how difficult or costly, is largely responsible for the horrible state of our families and communities. That is a hard truth to swallow. Nevertheless, it is the truth.

Every child needs Father Love. Every father can give it. It takes all of us doing everything we can to help them do it.

CHAPTER 14
Love Finds Joy in the Truth

We have been looking hard at the characteristics of love listed in 1 Corinthians 13 that show what love is not. Now we will turn our attention to the remaining of these sixteen love characteristics that focus on what love is, in the order that they were revealed to the Apostle Paul.

Acknowledging and finding joy in what is true is an essential characteristic of Father Love. Perhaps that is why Paul, in Philippians 4, encouraged Christians to meditate on the things that are true. He said, in part:

> *Rejoice in the Lord always. Again, I will say, rejoice! . . . Be anxious for nothing, but in everything by prayer and supplication, with thanksgiving, let your requests be made known to God; and the peace of God, which surpasses all understanding, will guard your hearts and minds through Christ Jesus. Finally, brethren, whatever things are true – meditate on these things. - Phil. 4:4–7*

When we consider how the Bible defines truth, we discover why it has the power to cause us to rejoice. The Lord Jesus Christ declared, "I am the way, the truth, and the life (John 14:6 NIV)." Those who know and love Jesus find their delight, their happiness, their exultation, their reason for celebration in Him. He is the truth and love finds its joy in Him. While others are searching for meaning and purpose in life, those who know God and who have

Chapter 14

surrendered their lives to His will find a joy that is supernatural.

It is a delight that defies human understanding. And it is a joy that the world, the tragedies, and the difficult circumstances of life cannot take away. Loving the God of truth is the recipe for a life of joy. Children need to see such joy in their fathers.

It is the indwelling Spirit of the Living God of Love that produces joy in the heart of the believer (see Gal. 5:22). It is that joy that sustains the child of God in difficult times. The prophet Nehemiah expressed this truth when he wrote under the anointing of Jehovah God, ". . . the joy of the LORD is your strength (Neh. 8:10 NIV)."

Christ Jesus *is* the Truth. We find our joy in Him, and He gives us power. If you are looking for joy, search for truth, because love finds its joy in the truth. The *ultimate truth* for the world today is the gospel of Jesus Christ. It is the simple good news that "Christ died for our sins according to the scriptures; and that He was buried, and that He rose again the third day according to the scriptures (1 Cor. 15:3-4)." Because of this extraordinary act of love, whoever believes in Him can have eternal life — a joy-filled eternal life.

This good news gives hope to all and joy to every man, woman, girl, and boy who obey the command to repent, are baptized in the name of Jesus, and are filled with the Holy Ghost. (see Acts 2:38)

According to Romans 1:16, the truth of the gospel is the power of salvation. The angels in heaven rejoice over every lost person who is saved because of the preaching of the gospel (see Luke 15:10 NIV). And so does every true child of God, because "love rejoiceth in the truth." The soul-saving truth of the gospel.

God's word *is* truth, and it brings joy to the hearts of those who love His Word. While many are searching for truth, others are claiming that all truth is relative. But there *is* an absolute truth. And this truth is the means for receiving joy in life.

Jesus Christ identified this absolute truth when He prayed this prayer for us: "Sanctify them by the truth: your word is truth (John 17:17 NIV)." Loving God and His Word the Holy Bible sanctifies (that is, sets us apart) from others. We are separated from those who reject, despise, or ignore His truth. We find joy in being set apart for His service.

King David wrote: "The statutes of the Lord are right, rejoicing the heart... more to be desired are they than gold, yea, than much fine gold; sweeter also than honey and the honey comb (Psalm 19:8a, 10)." God's word is perfect truth. Truth brings sweet joy to those who love it because "love rejoices in the truth."

When a father loves God's truth, he shares it with his children and others. He finds great joy in seeing others changed by it as he was. If you want the ultimate joy in life, embrace the Truth, the Lord Jesus Christ, and introduce your children to Him.

Those who love God, their children, and others discover great joy in seeing truth prevail. They get much satisfaction from seeing truth triumph in the affairs of men. That is why those who love their fellow man *work* for truth and justice on their behalf, defending the innocent and the falsely accused, laboring to overturn unjust laws, serving the poor and defenseless. The prophet Micah put succinctly what God wants of us, "He has showed you, O man, what is good. And what does the LORD require of you? To act justly and to love mercy and to walk humbly with your God (Mic. 6:8 NIV)."

Oh, that children would be witnesses to their father's profound

Chapter 14

love for God and their fellow man. That Father Love would be powerfully evidenced by the way fathers advocate for and serve their less fortunate neighbors. And that such love would be sufficiently contagious to infect the next generation.

The truth will ultimately and permanently prevail over evil and all kinds of injustice. Satan, who is the father of lies and *all* liars, shall be judged. Rev. 21:8 (KJV) warns ". . . all liars shall have their part in the lake which burn with fire and brimstone: which is the second death." Therefore, only those who are lovers of truth shall inherit the New Heavens and New Earth.

The book of Revelation also holds this promise for us in 21:27 (KJV): "And there shall in no wise enter into it anything that . . . maketh a lie, but they which are written in the Lamb's book of life." For eternity, those who love God and His word shall be praising and worshipping Him because, "love rejoices in the truth!" Each father's responsibility and privilege is to live in such a way that he can pass on the love of truth to his children. It is then up to each child to choose the truth for themselves.

A Quiet Father Love—John's Story

John had an "old school" father and grandfather, who both spoke love with actions but not words, and he says that's OK. Sure, the missing verbal confirmations were desired and needed. But John is now the head of a family charitable foundation today because of the fruits of his rearing.

"I have been very fortunate to grow up in the family I have, but we had our issues, too," he said. "My father was a very quiet man, who in my memory never told me that he loved me. But that was OK because everything he did told us he loved us."

John recalls one example of that unspoken love. "I had a paper route when I was a kid, and the years when we had big blizzards, my dad would be the one who woke me up early in the morning and took me around in his car delivering the papers. That was not only caring for but also working with me. And it helped me see that responsibility was important," he said.

John said his father was a protector, guider, and provider, but "a naturally reserved guy." "I look back and I don't think his father knew how to say that [I love you] either," he said. "So how can you blame your father for not saying it? Back then, it was all about actions. That was a time when dads were less inclined to show their emotions."

But those actions did demand something that is in short supply among the youth of today's America. "My grandpa [on his mom's side] was a typically stern grandfather—he demanded respect, but also was very quiet," John said. "You just knew there was an air of dignity around him. I don't think we even wanted to test him."

Chapter 14

He was all business, and his business was all him. "Bringing home the bacon was his way of letting us know that he loved us," John said. "You can have different styles and still be a good father. You gotta go with what God has given you."

John has learned that love is spelled R-E-S-P-E-C-T. "A big part of love is respect," he said. "That is something that is lost with kids today. There's a generational change that has taken place. You can see it in how we're dressed. In the informality of this generation, the opportunity for fathers to go deeper with kids is there. But it has to be balanced with respect. You don't want to be too 'friendly' with your kids, because you have to keep your authority. But you don't want to be afraid to talk to them either."

John admits that maintaining the balance is a struggle, but it is still crucial to effective fathering. John is thankful for the lessons he learned from his father figures and from his mother, who started and operated a local parent and infant center during his childhood. It showed him the overwhelming need of disadvantaged women and how they are related to fatherlessness.

"We always dealt with the most vulnerable women. And why were they in that situation? The man went missing or wasn't available," he said. "It is an interesting dynamic that thirty-five – forty years later, we're back to the core issue—the man."

John sees teaching men to be more relational is a key to overcoming many social ills. "I think it is a natural blind spot for a man," he said. "By nature, men are generally less intuitive, so they isolate. By nature, we're fixers." But still "old school," in a new world that demands new skills to fix things.

CHAPTER 15
Father Love is Nurturing

To nurture is to love, care for, and give attention to someone or something to promote flourishing. It is not a mother's responsibility only. Male nurturance is an essential tool for the healthy, holistic growth of a child. It is different from female nurturance, but one is not better than the other. The Creator's plan is for each child to experience both a balanced way.

When my oldest son Joseph was learning to walk, his mother (as moms are wired to do) was quick to rescue and comfort him when he'd fall. I was more inclined to let him fall on his fanny and then encourage him to try again. I'd say, "It's okay son, you're alright. Get up" then give hugs for trying. Children need both parental nurturing styles. That's why it is important that fathers are present during all those precious times, so their children can experience love, care, training, and attention, father-style.

But how does a father become a nurturer when he's never experienced male nurturance? That's an important question since so many males who are currently of childbearing age were raised in fatherless homes. This is where one-to-one mentoring, church fellowship, and dad groups can help. Fathers need each other to learn from and encourage one another.

Fatherhood programs can be a great resource for training fathers in male nurturance. I especially recommend bible-based curricula for Christ-following fathers. Bible-based father-focused programs I am aware of include Kingdom Dads, Legacy Dads, Care Net, and our own Father Love and Fathering Strong.

Fatherhood classes are a good start to combat father absence. But much more is needed on a societal scale to reduce the number of children who are growing up in homes where their fathers do not live, or who are not parenting well. Church-based fatherhood ministries have the potential to revive fatherhood within congregations, thus setting an example of culture changing in the rest of society. I will address that in Chapter 26 in this book.

Furthermore, even in father-present homes, often what children experience during formative years is aloofness, unmanaged anger, emotional absence, criticism, harshness, and rejection rather than male nurturance. Lacking any formal fatherhood training, many fathers I know simply decided to parent the opposite way their fathers behaved, and it worked for them.

Genuine Father Love is nurturing. To become a nurturer, one must love oneself enough to learn and practice self-nurture. That requires inspiration, introspection, insight, and intentionality.

Developing a Nurturing Father Love

INSPIRATION

Look Upward—Observe the Heavenly Father's examples of love that are found in the Bible. Consider the tender, merciful and faithful nature of the God's love. Seek to become more like Him. Ask Him for the Holy Spirit, which He promises will help His children to develop the fruit of the Spirit: love, joy, peace, longsuffering, kindness, goodness, faithfulness, gentleness and self-control (Gal. 5:22–23).

INTROSPECTION

Look Inward—Discover and work on healing your father wound. Think deeply about your childhood. Acknowledge any inner pain. Forgive those who have failed, neglected, abused, or hurt you in any way. Seek Christian counseling. Some men may desire professional counseling to help them heal the father wound caused by their childhood male nurturance deprivation.

INSIGHT

Look Around—Observe examples of nurturing fathers in your church or community. Seek out a pastor or an older man to learn from. Be willing to be mentored, gaining valuable teaching from your mentor's experiences. Join a fatherhood group or a fatherhood class for mutual learning and peer support.

INTENTIONALITY

Look Forward—Optimistically, believe that you will become a nurturer. Make a firm commitment to it. Start by taking care of your own spiritual, emotional, physical and all other needs. Promise yourself to give your child the nurturing Father Love you wish you'd experienced and then keep that promise.

Look Outward—Another example of intentionality is to purposefully extend Father Love to nurture a child who is not your own. Besides children, nurture your spouse and others in your life.

Chapter 15

Admonition: The Corrective Power of Nurturance

Along with the call for father nurturance is the need for its twin, admonition (or correction).

> *And, ye fathers, provoke not your children to wrath: but bring them up in the nurture and admonition of the Lord. –*
> *Ephesians 6:4 KJV*

The failure of a parent to both nurture and admonish a child can result in that child developing an attitude of wrath (anger).

We've all witnessed a child's public fit of rage with the mother at her wit's end as she struggles alone to handle the out-of-control child.

Father Love balanced with the tenderness of male nurturance and the firmness of male correction is essential to raising disciplined children. So, hug and kiss for sure, but don't neglect the occasional strong correction. Children really need it. Correction says, "Daddy loves you."

The most nurturing thing a father can do for his children is to cover them in Father Love.

CHAPTER 16
Love Bears All Things

Continuing to look at what love is, what does Paul mean in 1 Corinthians 13:7 (KJV) when he writes: "charity... beareth all things?" The original words may be translated: love *covers* all things. In our relationships, love covers over the faults of others. Listen to Apostle Peter about love:

> *And above all things have fervent love for one another, for 'love will cover a multitude of sins. - Pet. 4:8*

The word *fervent* means warmth of feeling and very earnest. So then, we are admonished to love each other warmly and sincerely. Our earnest love will cover over the minor failings and faults of another as far as it can do so. That is how God loves us.

Love "bears" or "covers over" all things. One who has the kind of love described in the Bible is not anxious to publicize the faults of his child, spouse, baby's mother, or anyone else. He does so only when obedience to God requires it. To the contrary, he is willing to forgive "seventy times seven," a biblical symbol for infinity, as Jesus instructs in Matthew 18:20-21. This creates in a child a sense of safety with his or her father.

Here is how Paul instructed the Colossian Christians:

> *Therefore, as the elect of God, holy and beloved, put on tender mercies, kindness, humility, meekness, longsuffering; bearing*

> *with one another, and forgiving one another, if anyone has a complaint against another; even as Christ forgave you, so you also must do. - Col. 3:12–14*

Yes, love bears all things by covering minor offenses and faults. As Christ forgave us, we are likewise to forgive those who trespass against us, including our children. Love is the more excellent way. It is the solution to lasting relationships and wise parenting. True God-lovers make a difference. When unbelievers see Christians loving each other and bearing with one another, it is a powerful witness. That is why Jesus said the world would know that we are His disciples if we have love for one for another.[li]

The person who loves God's way is unwilling to expose his child's, or anyone else's, minor faults by making them public. Love avoids bringing shame. Rather, love shields minor shortcomings from view. It bears or covers all things—even a "multitude of sins," as Peter put it. The person who loves others follows the golden rule, doing unto others as he would have them do unto him.

Husbands and wives who love each other deeply, honor each other by not exposing the other's minor faults as well—even to mutual friends—when doing so would cause hurt. Unmasking a loved one's flaws betrays trust and hinders intimacy. To do so to one's son or daughter angers and discourages them, which Scripture forbids:

> *Fathers, provoke not your children to anger, lest they be discouraged. - Col. 3:21 KJV*

Love Covers Over the Loved One's Blemishes

The loving mate does not expose the other's warts when it would be damaging to the marriage relationship. It would spoil the other's image in the eyes of others. I don't know about you, but I would prefer not to hear husbands and wives speaking disparagingly about each other. It makes me uncomfortable.

Love does not behave that way. It covers minor faults and protects its mate from hurt. It is the more excellent way and is the answer for happier marriages. Happier marriages produce happier parents. And happier parents raise happier and more loving children.

Just as marriage partners who love each other deeply do not disclose their mate's minor defects, the Christian who practices agape love protects his fellow believers and neighbors. He also refrains from listening to gossip about another's insignificant faults and inadequacies. It simply is not the loving thing to do. Besides, remember that your children are watching and learning from you. Likewise, to build and maintain a close relationship with your children, be careful not to embarrass them by revealing their faults to others.

Listen to Apostle Paul's instructions to the Ephesians when he writes,

> *Let no corrupt word proceed out of your mouth, but what is good for necessary edification, that it may impart grace to the hearers. And do not grieve the Holy Spirit of God, by whom you were sealed for the day of redemption. Let all bitterness, wrath, anger, clamor and evil speaking be put away from you, with all malice. And be kind to one another, tenderhearted-, forgiving one another, just as God in Christ forgave you. - Eph. 4:29–32*

Chapter 16

In love, we must speak only those things that will edify one another. Being kind and gracious to each other, let us overlook minor transgressions and forgive one another if any have cause to be offended. Because love bears all things, it is the solution for better relationships and better parenting.

Love Always Believes and Always Hopes

The father who truly loves is inclined toward faith, hope, and optimism. He is apt to believe the best for his children and their mother. Even when appearances and evidence suggest the worst, love still hopes for a good outcome. Loving God and believing His promises give reason for hopefulness.

> *And we know that all things work together for good to those who love God, to those who are the called according to His purpose.* - Rom. 8:28

When one's child has lost hope, the loving father has enough belief and hope to believe and hope *for* him or her. Father Love never gives up hope for a lost child. It means always believing that a child can change.

CHAPTER 17
Love Endures All Things and Never Fails

The last two of the sixteen 1 Corinthians 13 love characteristics emphasize that love is enduring and undefeatable.

The Bible assures us that love is the greatest of the fruit of the Spirit. It is at the core of the two greatest commandments given by our Lord Jesus Christ: Love God with all you've got and love your neighbor as yourself.[lii] 1 Corinthians 13:7 tells us that love endures all things. Because agape love is supernatural, it is strong enough to bear endlessly stressful days and lonely nights for the sake of its object. It is self-sacrificial. Agape is patient, even when provoked. It is no ordinary love. Love endures all things.

It bears up under misuse and unkindness for the cause of Christ. Love even perseveres through lies and insults. The supernatural nature of love holds firm when the fleshly human nature is ready to give up. Love stays though the relationship is strained. The perfect example of the enduring power of love is seen in God's love for His ancient people. Although the Israelites rebelled against Him time and again, Jehovah God, in His great love, continued to entreat them to return to Him.

And how many times have you and I disappointed Him? Yet He loves us still and forgives us when we repent. Consider also how His steadfast love for the lost moves Him to extend salvation to the worst of sinners—even those who curse Him. Yes, His love endures all things.

Agape love is the supernatural answer for many, if not most of the human relations problems in families, the workplace, churches and in the world. And fatherhood is no exception.

However, for love to be that remedy, it must be able to withstand all kinds of hardships. Paul, under the inspiration of the Holy Spirit, affirms that love endures *all* things. It is God's solution for us. We live in an age when people don't want to make long-term or lifetime commitments. When there are difficulties between friends, co-workers, church members, or even marriage partners, many people are ready to walk away from the relationship. Agape withstands tough times, weathers storms, and works to maintain essential relationships in the face of hardships. Love never gives up.

Isaac's Story of Determination

Tragically these days, some fathers walk away from their own children rather than love them enough to fight through every barrier placed in the way of their time with them. But there are many untold stories of enduring Father Love in action. Isaac's is one of them.

Isaac is a thirty-something African American father who participated in an Urban Light Ministries Fatherhood Program. Referred to the class by his county's Child Support Enforcement Agency, he became a changed man. The fire of his Father Love was stoked into a flame. After having fathered three children by three different women, he had since become a Christian. Wanting to become a better man and a more responsible parent, Isaac went to each of the mothers and apologized for his behavior.

Two forgave him and are providing regular access to his kids. However, one mother has refused and is denying Isaac time with his child. Determined to spend time regularly with each of his kids, Isaac is trying very hard, under extremely difficult circumstances. He had a low-paying job and three child support orders, which left him without enough money to adequately provide for himself. So he moved in with his mother in order to survive. He refused to give up. Isaac's story is an example of love never failing.

Wow! *Never* is a big word. But as we've seen, supernatural agape is perfectly dependable, faultless, and unfailing. Learning to love is learning to know Father God, because God *is* love. Practicing Father Love is the epitome of obedience to God's will. In loving us, God didn't give up on mankind, His children. He did for us what no one else could. He gave Himself totally, unconditionally, and sacrificially to redeem us from the curse of sin. Therefore, let us love one another in the same way, especially our children.[liii]

This is not optional for those who would be Christ's disciples. Jesus said: "This is my commandment, that you love one another as I have loved you (John 15:12)." In this we show the world that we are His disciples.[liv] It is not by our piety, programs, or prosperity. It is not by our evangelism, edifices, or endowments of the spirit. The proof of the authenticity of our Christianity is in our love for Him, as demonstrated by our love for each other. With God the Father and Christ the Son as our examples, let us love our children and their mothers, even to the extent of laying down our very lives.[lv]

We may feel at times in our life that we are completely defeated, but love is never defeated. Love never fails!

Father Love Never Gives Up!

During a Nurturing Fathers session being facilitated by Urban Light Ministries' fatherhood practitioner Donald "Woody" Walker at a correctional institution, a participant lamented out loud during a session that he would never be able to see or have any contact with his children because of their mother. Walker suggested that he not think or speak so negatively. "Our words are more powerful than many realize." Walker continued that we should try to describe things the way they are, not the way we fear they will be. "Never, ever give up," he stressed.

Many other participants disagreed emphatically with Walker's advice. However, the next week, the same man shared a letter he received from the mother of his children. The letter included photos of the children, an apology and an assurance that things would be different going forward. Needless to say, the father and the class got a wonderful lesson on the importance of "not giving up" that day.

Dad Is . . .

After writing all of the above about love, I read Roland Warren's wonderful book *Bad Dads of the Bible*[lvi] and was thrilled with his challenge for fathers to reread 1 Corinthians 13:4–7, replacing the words "love" and "it" with the word Dad. It would then read like this:

> Dad is patient. Dad is kind. Dad isn't jealous. Dad doesn't sing his own praises. Dad isn't arrogant.
>
> Dad isn't rude. Dad doesn't think about himself. Dad isn't irritable. Dad doesn't keep track of wrongs.

Chapter 17

Dad isn't happy when injustice is done, but Dad is happy with the truth. Dad never stops being patient, never stops believing, never stops hoping, and never gives up.

That's Father Love! Is that your commitment? Is it to love the way the Heavenly Father loves?

CHAPTER 18
Brad's Story of Father Love

After Brad's mother died, his alcoholic and workaholic father kicked him and his siblings out of the house. So it was that Brad became both motherless and fatherless at the tender age of thirteen.

Through the experience, Brad grew determined to never become a man who would under any circumstances abandon his children. Despite such an awful start, Brad did well in life. He married, had three children, and became successful in business. His job as a senior vice president in an agricultural business made it possible for him to afford an eight-bedroom country manor, complete with a four-bedroom guest house.

All appeared well as Brad, the loving father and husband, lived out the family life he had been deprived of as a child. Out of Christian compassion, Brad and his wife Janet took in more than fifty needy individuals over the years, providing free shelter and food in the family's guest quarters. Then, tragedy struck again.

Unbeknownst to Brad, Janet grew attracted to Bill, one of the male guests. She seduced him. Lying about going to visit out-of-state relatives, she took their children aged three, seven, and nine and ran off with Bill.

Chapter 18

When Brad discovered what had happened, he said it "felt like someone had taken a knife and stuck it through my chest." Resolute, Brad launched an all-out search for his children. His private detectives finally located them in another state. However, Brad's heartache was far from over.

In an effort to keep Brad from retrieving his children, Janet falsely accused him of sexually molesting their then seven-year-old daughter Chandra. She did this, knowing such an allegation would rally all the forces of the law to her side.

This began a seven-year struggle for Brad. Out of Father Love for his two sons and daughter, he has spent more than $2.5 million on lawyers, experts, and other legal expenses to be reunited with his children. Despite the enormous cost of battling not only his wife, but various county agencies, the court system, and the county judge, there has been no quit in Brad. All those forces have rallied to the mother's side, notwithstanding evidence of the falsity of the charge.

Undeterred, Brad is willing to do whatever is legal and necessary to be reunited with his children. His focus is on Chandra's emotional and spiritual healing. He is nearly inconsolable over the evil that has been done to her, having been coerced by her own mother into lying about such a horrible thing, and being forced to keep up the charade for seven years.

Amazingly, Brad does not hate Janet. In fact, he confesses his love for her still, despite all of this. His earnest prayer is for the mother of his children to come to repentance for what she has done, and for the restoration of Janet's relationship with God.

I've had many meetings with Brad, offering whatever prayers and other spiritual support I can provide to this tearful, emotionally distraught father in his heroic fight against such colossal odds. He has voluntarily enrolled in, and completed, Urban Light Ministries' fatherhood classes, devoting dozens of hours to developing male nurturance and relationship skills. He has maintained fellowship with a Christian men's group and attends church services for spiritual enrichment.

There have been victories along the way. Brad has been granted parenting time with each of his children. But he refuses to stop there. He wants his children to know the truth—that he would never have done the evil thing which he was accused of, and that he loves them too much to ever give up on them.

Further, Brad sees himself as being at the forefront of a fight for the rights of non-custodial parents everywhere. He knows that many such parents, most of whom are fathers, are being unfairly deprived of their God-given right to parent their children by systems that presume their guilt, make it next to impossible to prove their innocence, and deprive them of justice.

This small-town Caucasian man sees this as another great civil rights struggle, akin to the injustices suffered by blacks for hundreds of years in this country.

His fight for justice is not over, but recently Brad received the good news that he has been awarded full custody of Chandra. Yes, the very one that he was accused of molesting!

Brad's story inspired me to write the following.

Chapter 18

A Father's Manifesto

I am a father. I love my children. And with everything in me, I am determined to be their POPS.

I have what it takes to be their Protector, to watch over and keep them from dangers to their developing minds, bodies, souls, and spirits. I could never hurt them. I'd give my life for them. They are my children!

It's in me to be their Order Keeper . . . to make sure they have the security of boundaries established and enforced through a father's love for the regulation of their good conduct. They need me to help them grow up to become mature, responsible adults. I am their father!

I am committed to being their Provider . . . to do everything in my power to resource their material, emotional, intellectual, spiritual, and every other need to the best of my ability. If I have to go without food, shelter, and clothing, my kids will have what they need. They are my children!

I yearn to be their Stabilizer . . . to be their anchor during the storms of life, so that no matter what happens, and though others come and go, they may know that my love endures. I will be there. I am their POPS!

I am a father. I endeavor to love, respect and honor their mother. I know it is supremely important to my children that they know and see that. My children need both their parents caring for them. I will do all that I can to co-parent my children with their mother. But if she refuses our children that blessing, I will not relent. I insist on being a major part of my kids' lives and having them as part of my life. They are my children!

I don't need the government or anyone else to interfere with, regulate or manage my fathering. I accept full responsibility for my children. They are mine. I will not quit. I will not be deterred, distracted or discouraged. I am fighting for a cause greater than myself. I am their father! They are my children!

No agency, social worker or judge can love my children the way I do. I know what's in their best interests. I am their dad and I will stand up for them against all odds.

I'm not perfect. Yes, like you, I've made mistakes. But I promise to learn and to grow to be the nurturing father my children need, taking full advantage of every resource available to me. I am their father!

If I am given the gift of children not of my flesh, I will love them just the same. I have a father's heart, and it beats even for those children not in my home. If I can do anything to help those, I will do that as well. I am a father!

And when my children are grown and out on their own, I am still POPS. And if God is willing, I will be there for my children's children, and the next generation after that.

I am blessed. I am determined to fulfill this higher calling given to me by my Creator. I am a father!

    The love of a father for his children is a tremendous force for good. As a society, we should be doing everything we can to encourage and support, rather than to erect barriers for fathers in their parental responsibilities. Father Love is indeed a powerful resource that every child needs.

Chapter 18

Fathers Matter

In Brad's story, the children had everything they needed . . . their own bedrooms, plenty of food, and all the necessities of life for growing children. After Janet took the children, they soon ended up homeless and destitute. *Of course, not all families' circumstances and how the children come to be fatherless are the same. Often, the father has abandoned the children, as was the case with young Bradley and his siblings' father.*

As stated earlier in this book, clearly, children are better off in two-parent households. Children living in married-couple families consistently experience significantly lower poverty rates compared to children in single-parent households, particularly those headed by a female householder. Based on the U.S. Census Bureau's 2024 report on 2023 data, the poverty rate for children under 18 living in **married-couple families** was **6.4%**. In stark contrast, the poverty rate for children living in **female-householder families (no spouse present)** was **29.7%**. This difference of over 23 percentage points highlights the financial stability that married-couple families, on average, provide. This disparity is a key reason why discussions about poverty often include the importance of family structure.

While it is important that communities become more effective at addressing the father-absence crisis and all its horrible consequences for children, I am convinced that we must simultaneously engage in an all-out effort to embrace and nurture Father Love. It's simple: More Father Love being practiced means better outcomes for children and lower costs to society for fighting poverty. But there are forces in our society that, despite the truth of all the aforementioned, actively work against fatherhood.

CHAPTER 19
Doing Battle for Fathers and Families

Have you wondered just how it is that the institutions of fatherhood and family are in such trouble?

There are many societal and cultural developments that have contributed to the breakdown of the family. Experts in those fields have written extensively about those topics. But there is a spiritual factor not often mentioned.

In Ephesians 6:12, Paul told us that there is an unseen war going on. He said, "For we do not wrestle against flesh and blood, but against principalities, against powers, against the rulers of the darkness of this age, against spiritual hosts of wickedness in the heavenly places."

The 2015 Alex and Stephen Kendrick movie *War Room*[lvii] does a good job of calling attention to this very real conflict. The warfare against the family is being waged by Satan, the angel who made himself the chief enemy of God.

He did that when he rejected the Father's love out of his own selfish pride. He has enlisted an army of other evil, fallen angels that share this hatred of God. The Lord Jesus Christ revealed the devil's strategy as recorded in John 10:10: "The thief does not come except to steal, and to kill, and to destroy." The devil's aim is to

Chapter 19

destroy the human race—God's crowning achievement in the material world He created.

Satan's strategy is to target the very foundation of mankind, the family. Because the Creator established the man as head of the family, Satan attacks the man to destroy the family. That is elementary in warfare: Cut off the head and the body will die.

The war on the family began in the Garden of Eden.[lviii] Employing a lie as a weapon, Satan persuaded the first woman, Eve, to disobey her husband, Adam's clear instruction from God not to eat from the tree in the midst of the garden.

The Garden of Eden was filled with food-laden plants. The Creator had reserved that one tree for Himself. Tragically, Adam went along with the rebellion and also ate the forbidden fruit. That act of rejection of the Creator's authority and sovereign rule was a game-changer. The close relationship that Adam had enjoyed with Father God, his Creator, was now severed. God's earthly family was now estranged from Him.

As the appointed head, Adam had the responsibility of loving and leading his family. Instead he chose to join Eve in her rebellion against His Creator. It was a failure to love his wife enough to correct her bad behavior. Even worse, Adam and his wife's defiance was a repudiation of the Father's love. After all, the test of one's love of God is obedience. Jesus told His disciples, "If you love Me, keep My commandments (John 14:15 NIV)."

Satan enjoyed a victory in this battle, but the war over the human family was only beginning. In sentencing the devil for deceiving Eve, God told him that he would ultimately be defeated by a male descendant of the woman.[lix]

We know that promised Victor to be the Lord Jesus Christ, the Son of God.[lx] He is the perfect Second Adam sent from God, whose sacrificial death on a cross takes away the sin of the world.[lxi] In three days He was raised to life in total victory over Satan, death, and the grave.

That's great news for you! You can receive the salvation He offers by simply believing in Him.

If you confess with your mouth the Lord Jesus and believe in your heart that God has raised Him from the dead, you will be saved. For with the heart one believes unto righteousness, and with the mouth confession is made unto salvation. - Rom. 10:9–10

In the meantime, the war to destroy the family rages on. The consequences of Adam's fall were horrific immediately. The first family was driven from the garden to lives filled with sorrow, struggle, and pain, and then to die. Their son Cain murdered their other son, Abel, in a jealous fit of rage. As the centuries have passed, every manner of trial and tribulation has pummeled the institutions of fatherhood and family.

Engaging the Enemy

It is no ordinary conflict. We are engaged in a different kind of warfare. To do effective battle in this warfare, spiritual weaponry is needed. *"For we do not wrestle against flesh and blood (Eph. 6:12a)."*

The battle is "... against principalities, against powers, against the rulers of the darkness of this age, against spiritual hosts of wickedness in the heavenly places (Eph. 6:12b)." It's evil that is entrenched in seemingly impregnable fortresses. What are those fortresses? Paul put it this way as he was moved by the Holy Spirit while teaching the Christians at Corinth:

Chapter 19

For though we walk in the flesh, we do not war according to the flesh. For the weapons of our warfare are not carnal but mighty in God for pulling down strongholds, casting down arguments and every high thing that exalts itself against the knowledge of God, bringing every thought into captivity to the obedience of Christ, and being ready to punish all disobedience when your obedience is fulfilled. - 2 Cor. 10:3-6

The Strongholds of 2 Corinthians 10:4

These strongholds are well-fortified, invisible, wicked platforms from which the family and everything godly are attacked. They are described as:

- Arguments
- Every high thing that exalts itself against the knowledge of God

These are theories and deceptive fantasies that can lead us astray from the truth as revealed in God's Word and as taught by the Holy Spirit. So, this is a war against intellectual conceits, barriers of pride, and imposing defenses erected by proud men who are bent on turning people away from seeking and serving God.

These arguments are entrenched in culture today. Publicly disagreeing with them draws the ire of some people who hold a secular worldview. The attacks can be vicious, making these ungodly beliefs seem like impregnable fortresses. In doing battle, we must take an unwavering stand for the truth of God's Word, no matter the consequences. We must "[t]est all things; hold fast what is good (1 Thess. 5:21)."

To overthrow these fortresses, spiritual weapons are needed. With them, we are able to destroy every subtle, tricky, false argument that opposes the Gospel of Jesus Christ and rears its proud head against the knowledge of God.

Taking Thoughts Captive

The first battle front in spiritual warfare is internal.

Were you told that you are worthless, that your kids don't need you and you should just move on with your life? Have you believed the lie that fathers are not as important as mothers to children? Do you struggle with low self-esteem, feeling that your past mistakes have disqualified you from being a parent to your children? Do you believe that being financially challenged means you have nothing of value to give your kids?

These negative, untrue thoughts have the potential of keeping you from reaching your potential as a father. It is vital that you know and believe the truth about God's love, mercy and grace toward you. Jesus said, "and you shall know the truth, and the truth shall make you free (John 8:31-32)."

With God's help, you can take control of all that "stinkin' thinkin'" and make your thoughts conform to God's Word. Then, you will indeed be free to become the man God intended.

The Battleground

We are indeed in a spiritual struggle, and the battleground is the human mind.

> *So, letting your sinful nature control your mind leads to death. But letting the Spirit control your mind leads to life and peace. For the sinful nature is always hostile to God. It never did obey God's laws, and it never will.* - Rom. 8:6-7 NLT

Chapter 19

Put another way, the mind of a human being is either controlled by the Spirit of God, or it is unreceptive to God, and therefore does whatever the fallen human nature dictates.

The enemy, Satan — whom the Bible calls the God of this world — has blinded the minds of unbelievers so that they cannot see the light of the Gospel. Therefore, they are blind to the glory of Christ, who is the very image of God (see 2 Cor. 4:3-5).

Satan's clever lies deceive people and make it harder for them to receive the Gospel of Jesus Christ, which robs them of life and peace. The devil would have you believe that you are worthless to your children and incapable of Father Love. In this way, children are deprived of the male nurturance and the many resources that every child needs from their father.

Listen to what Jesus said to those who rejected His truth:

Why is my language not clear to you? Because you are unable to hear what I say. You belong to your father, the devil, and you want to carry out your father's desire. He was a murderer from the beginning, not holding to the truth, for there is no truth in him. When he lies, he speaks his native language, for he is a liar and the father of lies. - John 8:43-44 NIV

If you are a born-again child of God, you are at war against powerful, wicked, unseen forces. They are "principalities, against powers, against the rulers of the darkness of this age, against spiritual hosts of wickedness in the heavenly places (Eph. 6:12)." But, what exactly are these principalities and powers and rulers we are up against as we endeavor to be the kind of person, spouse, parent and citizen that God wants us to be?

The enemy

Our struggle is against evil spiritual forces. That is, governing authorities of empires that control and rule the darkness around us. This war is not against human beings. It is not a battle with the mother of your child, the child support enforcement agency or the family court. It is much bigger than that. It is a struggle against the unseen principalities of spiritual darkness.

What is a principality?

A principality is an area of jurisdiction ruled by a prince. In Ephesians 2:2, Paul, with insight given by the Spirit of God, calls Satan "the prince of the power of the air (NKJV)." In the New Living Translation, this is rendered "the commander of the powers of the unseen world." We know that his jurisdiction is among mankind because that passage of Scripture goes on to identify the power of the air as the spirit that is at work in the world today. Satan is the spirit at work in the hearts of those who refuse to obey God.

There is an overriding attitude, or way of thinking that prevails in today's world and it is powerful. It is inspired by God's chief enemy, Satan, who wants to destroy humanity. And he knows that the way to do that is by dismantling the family. This evil power of the air is potent enough to even infect the church. Paul wrote to Timothy about how this ungodly way of thinking and living would impact the world, including religious people as time goes on:

> *But know this, that in the last days perilous times will come: For men will be lovers of themselves, lovers of money, boasters, proud, blasphemers, disobedient to parents, unthankful, unholy, unloving, unforgiving, slanderers, without self-control, brutal,*

> *despisers of good, traitors, headstrong, haughty, lovers of pleasure rather than lovers of God, having a form of godliness but denying its power. And from such people turn away! - 2 Tim. 3:1–5*

Notice how selfish, materialistic, anti-family, ungrateful, prideful, mean, anti-God, and hypocritical this dark spirit is. It is the same attitude that Satan has. But he is not alone in this evil domination over rebellious people's thinking.

Other powers and rulers

Satan and a horde of fallen angels are the "powers" that possess control over a dark domain. They are "rulers" over all humans who dwell in spiritual darkness. They use people as pawns in this war.

In fact, Satan's wicked empire is the headquarters of everything evil. Thankfully, Jesus declared in John 16:11 that Satan, the prince of this world, is judged. "Judgment will come because the ruler of this world has already been judged (John 16:11 NLT)."

> *The devil knows that he is headed for the abyss. But he is angry and wants to take with him to eternal banishment as many people as he can. The Bible describes him as a lion stalking prey to devour. "Be sober, be vigilant; because your adversary the devil walks about like a roaring lion, seeking whom he may devour (1 Pet. 5:8)."*

In John 10:10, Jesus likened Satan to a thief coming to kill, to steal, and to destroy. However, you don't have to be his victim. God has provided the spiritual weapons we discussed earlier. We desperately need this divine armament to aid us in this spiritual warfare for fathers and family.

CHAPTER 20
The Divine Armor

When you are going to war for your family, it is important for fathers to dress properly and have the best weapons.

Listen to these inspiring words to the Christians at Ephesus:

> *Finally, my brethren, be strong in the Lord, and in the power of His might. Put on the whole armor of God, that ye may be able to stand against the wiles of the devil. (Eph. 6:10-11)*

The Apostle Paul here exhorts his Christian brothers and sisters to be strengthened in the Lord, to recognize that our strength comes from God and that it is His mighty power that enables our victory in the battle for control of our minds. Then, Paul instructed us to put on the *whole* armor of God.

We need the complete armor the Lord provides in order to withstand the onslaught of Satan's evil strategies against our families. When he confronts us with lies and temptations, assails us with sickness and disease, attacks us by stealing what is ours, we must be wearing all the armor of the Lord in order to be victorious.

Satan attacks with all manner of wicked schemes and cunning methods designed to discourage, disgruntle, depress, and defeat dads and all devoted children of God. It is truly a battle for your mind. So, in Ephesians 6:13-17 Paul urges us to, "put on the whole armor of God," so that when evil comes against us and our families we may be able to stand strong in the power of God's might. Then, having succeeded in resisting all of the enemy's attacks, we may be found still on our feet—holding our ground—victorious in battle.

In spiritual warfare, we need the armor of God... all of it. Roman soldiers in Jesus's day donned a complete suit of armor before going into battle. Likewise, when preparing for war against our enemies, we need the full armor. What are the parts of this spiritual armament?

The Girdle of Truth (Eph. 6:14)

Jesus said to the hypocritical religious leaders of His day who had made themselves enemies of God,

> *You are of your father the devil, and the desires of your father you want to do. He was a murderer from the beginning, and does not stand in the truth, because there is no truth in him. When he speaks a lie, he speaks from his own resources, for he is a liar and the father of it. - John 8:44*

To defeat Satan's lies, we need to wear God's truth as a belt around our waist. When Satan attacks, armed with knowledge of the truth, we are able to answer the way Jesus did during His temptation in the wilderness: "It is written."

When you know the truth, it sets you free from the enemy's clever deceptions (John 8:32). When the devil and his agents—human or demonic—come against you with temptations to sin, you will resist because you have hidden the word in your heart (Ps. 119:11).

In John 17:17, it is recorded that Jesus prayed to the Father for His disciples. "Sanctify them by the truth; your word is truth." The Father sanctifies us—sets us apart—so that we can be useful in His service, and to our families—by His truth.

The Breastplate of Righteousness

This alludes to the truth that righteousness is a protection. The breastplate covers the heart.

The Bible identifies the devil as "the accuser of our brethren (Rev. 12:10)." As the father of lies, he will try to dishearten you with this deceitful tactic so that you will stop serving God and walk away from your children and family—leaving them more vulnerable to him.

When we endeavor to always do the right thing, our enemies' accusations against us ring hollow. When we do the right thing by our families, work for justice for the oppressed, and seek to rescue the needy, we stand as a witness for our loving Lord. And we stand in stark opposition to Satan and the evil, unrighteous, oppressive darkness over which he rules.

Of course, we have no goodness of our own. All the decent things we do are like filthy rags in comparison to God's uprightness (see Isa. 64:6). It is the righteousness of Jesus Christ that is imputed to us upon salvation that makes it possible for the Father to consider us virtuous.

How did this happen? In an amazing exchange, all of our sin was transferred by Father God to His Son on the cross, and His righteousness was imparted to us at His sacrificial death. "For He made Him who knew no sin to be sin for us, that we might become the righteousness of God in Him (2 Cor. 5:21)."

Chapter 20

Wow! Jesus took all of my sin upon Himself and died for me. Now I am justified by faith. What does that mean? It is just as if I'd never sinned. He gave me grace (a gift I don't deserve) and mercy (withheld the punishment that I deserve). And He did the same for you!

Born-again Christians have believed and received this wonderful truth by faith and are saved. Have you? If so, you know that you are approved by God. No matter what the enemy hurls at you, you know you will withstand it. His lies and every other attack will bounce off your breastplate and will never reach your heart. Stand your ground . . . confident that you will prevail in your commitment to loving parenting and marriage.

Good News Shoes

The full armor of God includes "having shod your feet with the preparation of the gospel of peace (Eph. 6:15–16)." We put on shoes that are appropriate for the planned activity . . . working, walking, hiking, running, golf, baseball, basketball, dancing. Likewise, for spiritual warfare, let each of us put on a ready mind to share this wonderful hope with others, starting with our families.

Isa. 52:7 (NIV) declares: "How beautiful on the mountains are the feet of those who bring good news, who proclaim peace, who bring good tidings, who proclaim salvation, who say to Zion. Your God reigns!" Be ready to carry the light of the gospel into the darkness. With a heart full of Father Love, endeavor to communicate the Gospel of Jesus Christ to your children in a way that they will understand it and will desire their own relationship with God.

The Shield of Faith

Satan wants to undermine, even destroy, your confidence in God. To combat him, you need faith.

The Roman soldier's shield was designed to be light enough to carry in one hand, but large enough to cover its wielder's entire body. That way, whatever projectile was launched would not hit the soldier and injure him. Likewise in spiritual warfare, faith is able to protect you from everything the enemy hurls at you. No weapon formed against you will prosper. (see Isa. 54:17)

What is faith? "Now faith is the substance of things hoped for, the evidence of things not seen (Heb. 11:1)."

Faith is a gift from God that enables one to have confidence that what God promises will happen. It is being so sure that things will come to pass just as He said they would that one takes action in obedience to His Word.

This is an invaluable protection in spiritual battle. The enemy will try to cause you to doubt God's Word. He will attempt to get you to start questioning God's love for you and His presence with you. With faith as a shield, you will resist his efforts against you and your family. Father God will be delighted as you stand firm in the faith despite all of Satan's attacks. "But, without faith, it is impossible to please Him (Heb. 11:6)."

Wield your shield!

Chapter 20

The Helmet of Salvation

In battle, the enemy knows that if he cuts off the head, the body will die. Satan wants to infiltrate your mind; that is your thinking, and your attitude. Remember, he wants to deceive you.

So, he comes against you with all kinds of machinations that are calculated to defeat you as the God-ordained head of your family. He will even tell you that you are not really saved. He will tell you that because you have made this or that mistake, committed a sin, failed at something or another that you've blown it . . . that you'll never measure up as a father or husband.

Protect yourself by having unshakeable confidence in your salvation. Wear it like a helmet. Remind yourself of the promises in the eighth chapter of Romans:

There is therefore now no condemnation to those who are in Christ Jesus, who do not walk according to the flesh, but according to the Spirit. - Rom. 8:1

And we know that all things work together for good to those who love God, to those who are the called according to His purpose. - Rom. 8:28

And these in verses in Romans 8:33-37:

> *Who shall bring a charge against God's elect? It is God who justifies. Who is he who condemns? It is Christ who died, and furthermore is also risen, who is even at the right hand of God, who also makes intercession for us. Who shall separate us from the love of Christ? Shall tribulation, or distress, or persecution, or famine, or nakedness, or peril, or sword? As it is written: "For*

> *Your sake we are killed all day long; We are accounted as sheep for the slaughter." Yet in all these things we are more than conquerors through Him who loved us.*

Be confident that, because of God's love and the intercession of Christ, nothing can separate you from God's love—no matter what comes against you. God will make it all work out for you. You are more than a conqueror in Christ. Wear this blessed assurance as a protection for your mind—as a soldier wears headgear. Put on the helmet of salvation.

The Sword of the Spirit

The armor of God is not complete without a sword. Obviously, for spiritual warfare, this is not just any sword. The sword of the Spirit—with a capital "S"—is a symbol of the Word of God, the Bible.

To do battle against Satan's lies, God has provided His written truth. It is these truths that protect the soldier of God against false arguments which are raised up in opposition to God—no matter how popular they are. The truth will always win in the end. It is more powerful than the lie.

In setting the example for us, Jesus, when attacked by Satan in the desert, spoke the truth to defeat his lies (see Luke 4:1-12). Three times, in response to Satan's attempts to entice Him into sin, Jesus countered with "it is written." This was enough to cause the devil to leave Jesus alone for a while.

Knowing what the Word says is a protection against deception. Hide the word of God in your heart that you might not be tricked into sinning against God (see Ps. 119:11). The Word has everything

Chapter 20

you need for life and godliness and for spiritual battle (see 2 Pet. 1:3).

Use this powerful weapon to teach your children God's ways. They too need the sword of the Spirit. The sooner they learn to use it, the better.

Prayer

In concluding his teaching on the whole armor of God, Paul urged the believers at Ephesus to "...pray in the Spirit at all times and on every occasion. Stay alert and be persistent in your prayers for all believers everywhere (Eph. 6:18 NLT)."

Prayer is an indispensable weapon in spiritual warfare. We need to continually pray for one another as we are all engaged in this struggle against Satan, the world that's under his control and our own fallen flesh. Pray for other fathers everywhere, because father absence is an international crisis.

In our intercession for all Christians worldwide, and likewise for families, we don't know exactly what to pray on their behalf. Therefore, Paul exhorts us to pray in the Spirit—trusting God to interpret our prayer.

> *In the same way, the Spirit helps us in our weakness. We do not know what we ought to pray for, but the Spirit himself intercedes for us with groans that words cannot express. And he who searches our hearts knows the mind of the Spirit, because the Spirit intercedes for the saints in accordance with God's will. - Rom. 8:26-27 NIV*

Pray regularly *for* your children, your family, and for fathers and families everywhere. Pray regularly *with* your children and family.

Victory is yours!

The outcome of this war against fathers and families is not in doubt for the child of God. No, in all these things "we are more than conquerors through him who loved us (Rom. 8:37)." Praise God that we shall overcome "by the blood of the Lamb and by the word of (our) testimony (Rev. 12:11)."

You, too, can have this confidence. The first step to prevailing in the war for your family is to be saved. It is a supernatural war, and only supernatural power will win it. Only His born-of-the-Spirit children have that spiritual power residing within them. You can have it as well. Become a child of God by receiving Jesus Christ as your Savior. Until you've done that, you've already lost.

Victory in the war for your family requires faith in, and obedience to, the Word of God. Read it, study it, obey it, and share it. You shall be more than a conqueror through Christ Jesus whose love is more powerful than anything known to mankind.

> *And I am convinced that nothing can ever separate us from God's love. Neither death nor life, neither angels nor demons, neither our fears for today nor our worries about tomorrow – not even the powers of hell can separate us from God's love. No power in the sky above or in the earth below – indeed, nothing in all creation will ever be able to separate us from the love of God that is revealed in Christ Jesus our Lord. - Rom. 8:38-39 NLT*

Chapter 20

CHAPTER 21
A Biblical Story of Father Love in Action

In the fifteenth chapter of Luke, Jesus gave a parable about a father that exhibited Father Love for his selfish and foolish son.[lxii] Known as the story of "The Prodigal Son," a modern adaption of the story could go like the following.

The Grace of Father Love

A successful small business owner had two sons. He loved them both and was training them in the family business to eventually take over after his retirement. However, the younger son grew impatient and asked his father to give him his share of the inheritance now. It must have broken the father's heart that his son had no interest in keeping the family business going but only cared about what he could get out of it now. The younger son gave no thought about the family legacy, helping his brother or preserving the business for the security of his own children. He wasn't even willing to wait for his father's passing.

Nonetheless, the father's love for his son moved him to do as his son asked. Perhaps, he was hoping that the young man would come to his senses. So, he gave the younger son his inheritance. This was a father's grace in action... giving what was not deserved.

Chapter 21

The Grace and Mercy of Father Love

Not long after he received his loot, the younger son took it all and headed out of town. In a city far away, he partied hard. He wasted it all on every kind of extravagance. He blew every dime!

After his fortune was all gone, hard times hit. He became homeless and hungry. Out of desperation, he went to work for a farmer, feeding his hogs. He was so hungry, he would have eaten the pods that the hogs were eating, but his employer wouldn't give him any.

Finally, a light came on his hard head. He thought, "What am I doing here? My dad's employees live a lot better than this. They've got more than enough food. And here I am starving to death! I'm going home and confess to him that I've sinned against God and him. I'll tell him I'm not worthy to be his son anymore and ask him to let me come back to work as one of his employees." So, he headed for home.

The father, having been waiting, watching and hoping for his son's return, spotted him in the distance. Compassion for his long-awaited son drove the father to run to meet him. He hugged his boy and kissed him on the forehead. The sobbing young man said, "I've sinned against God and against you. I'm not worthy to be your son anymore, but please . . ." But before he could finish his prepared speech and ask his father to give him a job, the father took out his cellphone and called his foreman. He instructed him to have his employees go to his closet to get his son some clean clothes to change into.

"Bring my best for him. Tell my chef to prepare a huge dinner. Make it filet mignon! I thought my son was dead, but he's alive. I feared I'd lost him forever, but he's home. It's party time!" This was a father's mercy in action . . . not giving what was deserved.

The Biblical Story of Father Love in Action

After they had feasted to their hearts' content, they were singing and dancing to the music. The older son, who was out working in the field, heard it. He asked one of the hired hands what was going on. He told him, "Your brother is back. Your father is so happy to have him safely home that he served-up his best beef."

The older brother was so angry that he refused to come to the party. The father came out to his son and pleaded with him to come inside and join the celebration. But the senior son answered, "Look Dad, I've been here faithfully working for you all these years. I've not disobeyed you in any way. Yet you never threw a party for me and my friends. But this other son of yours left us and blew your money on prostitutes, and as soon as he shows up here, you give him the best steaks we've got?!"

The older brother was willing to give neither grace nor mercy to his younger, wayward sibling. I can understand his feeling, can't you? I'm sure big bro was thinking, "What a selfish, foolish brat he's been. Now he's back, as if what he'd done is fine. And I'm supposed to join the party for him?"

The father said to his elder son, "Look, because you have always been here with me, everything I have is yours. The business, the house ... everything! He is your brother. Come on and help me celebrate his return home. We thought he was dead ... lost forever. Be happy, son. Your brother is alive!"

Father Love has enough grace to give gifts to even the most ungrateful of children. It has the patience to wait for the return of the wayward. It is sufficiently merciful to withhold punishment when it is deserved. And Father Love is also wise enough to gently reprove the faithful when they become self-righteous.

Chapter 21

Filled with Father Love, let us dads look to Our Heavenly Father for instruction and guidance for parenting our children well into their young adult lives. After all, fathering is for life.

CHAPTER 22
The Creator's Father Love

Since the God of the Bible *is* love[lxiii], it only makes sense to look to Him for the perfect example of Father Love in action.

What are some of His characteristics with respect to His parenting of His human children? Below are just a few.

He is a Provider and Order Keeper

The Creator provided all the first couple needed, including love, companionship, challenging and fulfilling work, food, shelter, and safety. He intended the male and female to be united for life as they fulfilled their responsibility to fill the earth with their offspring while taking care of them, the earth, and its creatures. Adam and Eve were to follow God's example as providers.

> *Then God said, "Let Us make man in Our image, according to Our likeness; let them have dominion over the fish of the sea, over the birds of the air, and over the cattle, over all the earth and over every creeping thing that creeps on the earth." So God created man in His own image; in the image of God He created him; male and female He created them. Then God blessed them, and God said to them, "Be fruitful and multiply; fill the earth and subdue it; have dominion over the fish of the sea, over the birds of the air, and over every living thing that moves on the earth." And God said, "See, I have given you every herb that yields seed which is on the face of all the earth, and every tree whose fruit yields seed; to you it shall be for food. Also, to every*

Chapter 22

> *beast of the earth, to every bird of the air, and to everything that creeps on the earth, in which there is life, I have given every green herb for food;" and it was so. Then God saw everything that He had made, and indeed it was very good. So the evening and the morning were the sixth day. God set everything in order.*
> *- Gen. 1:26-31*

The first couple was charged with keeping that order. Having been created first, Adam was charged with leadership of the family. Eve was given the great honor and responsibility of becoming the mother of all living. As God is the Divine Order Keeper of all that He has created, together Adam and Eve were to be the order keepers over God's earthly establishment.

He is a Teacher and Guide

Because He loves us, the Heavenly Father has given His earthly children instructions. Those who trust Him and follow His teachings are guided throughout life by the wisdom contained in His Word.

Likewise, we earthly fathers have the responsibility of teaching and guiding our children. The wisest man who has ever lived, King Solomon of ancient Israel, gave the following teachings to his son:

> *My son, do not forget my law, But let your heart keep my commands; For length of days and long life and peace they will add to you. Let not mercy and truth forsake you; Bind them around your neck, Write them on the tablet of your heart, and so find favor and high esteem In the sight of God and man. Trust in the LORD with all your heart, and lean not on your own*

understanding; In all your ways acknowledge Him, And He shall direct your paths. - Prov. 3:1–6

He Is a Loving Disciplinarian

Out of love for His children, the Heavenly Father corrects His people when they need it. The Old Testament Scriptures are replete with accounts of Jehovah God's disciplinary actions against Israel after disobeying Him.

We earthly dads serve our children well when, in love, we provide timely reproof. It is our responsibility to love our kids enough to correct them when they need it.

My son, do not despise the chastening of the LORD, Nor detest His correction; For whom the LORD loves He corrects, Just as a father the son in whom he delights. - Prov. 3:11–12

He Is a Protector

God the Father watches over His children who trust in Him to protect them from harm. He has assigned angels for the protection of His children.[lxiv]

A loving, earthly father gladly accepts the privilege of being his child's guardian against physical, spiritual, emotional, and every other kind of harm.

Because you have made the LORD, who is my refuge, Even the Most High, your dwelling place, No evil shall befall you, Nor shall any plague come near your dwelling; For He shall give His angels charge over you, To keep you in all your ways. - Psalm 91:9–11

Chapter 22

He Is a Rewarder

The Creator God loves to reward His children for their obedience. He has put the law of sowing and reaping into place.[lxv] As we go about doing good things, His blessings are experienced daily. And he has guaranteed eternal rewards for those who faithfully serve Him. A father who rewards his child's good behaviors will get more of them.

> *But without faith it is impossible to please Him, for he who comes to God must believe that He is, and that He is a rewarder of those who diligently seek Him. - Heb. 11:6*

He Is Caring

The Heavenly Father demonstrates His concern by inviting His children to bring all their anxieties to Him. Jesus bids His followers to come to Him with their burdens with the promise of relief.[lxvi]

In the same way, loving dads are available to their children and encourage open communication about everything that concerns them.

> *Therefore humble yourselves under the mighty hand of God, that He may exalt you in due time, casting all your care upon Him, for He cares for you. - 1 Pet. 5:6–7*

The Loving Parent's Heart of Jesus Christ

Jesus is filled with compassion for His wayward children. He came in human flesh to seek those who have strayed, giving His life to save them.[lxvii]

Following God's example, loving earthly fathers have compassionate concern for their children and will do whatever is necessary to secure their well-being.

> O Jerusalem, Jerusalem, the one who kills the prophets and stones those who are sent to her! How often I wanted to gather your children together, as a hen gathers her chicks under her wings, but you were not willing! - Matt. 23:37

The Holy Spirit Is Helper and Teacher

God is ever present with His children and is available to assist us in every circumstance. He doesn't simply tell us what to do, He shows us the way! In a like manner, good dads do all they can to help their kids succeed in life—not by doing everything for them, but by showing them the way.

> But the Helper, the Holy Spirit, whom the Father will send in My name, He will teach you all things, and bring to your remembrance all things that I said to you. - John 14:26

All these characteristics of Father Love are essential for an earthly father to develop if he wants to be the kind of father that God is to His children.

The Heavenly Father's Love for His Son

The Provision of Godly Parents

Father God, before His Son left Heaven to take on human flesh to rescue lost mankind from eternal separation from Him, lovingly made preparations on earth. He chose two parents to care for Him. Luke 1:26–45 tells a lot about His soon-to-be human mother.

Chapter 22

Starting with verse 26, the Bible says:

> *Now in the sixth month the angel Gabriel was sent by God to a city of Galilee named Nazareth, to a virgin betrothed to a man whose name was Joseph, of the house of David. The virgin's name was Mary. And having come in, the angel said to her, "Rejoice, highly favored one, the Lord is with you; blessed are you among women!" But when she saw him, she was troubled at his saying, and considered what manner of greeting this was. Then the angel said to her, "Do not be afraid, Mary, for you have found favor with God. And behold, you will conceive in your womb and bring forth a Son, and shall call His name JESUS. He will be great, and will be called the Son of the Highest; and the Lord God will give Him the throne of His father David. And He will reign over the house of Jacob forever, and of His kingdom there will be no end." Then Mary said to the angel, "How can this be, since I do not know a man?" And the angel answered and said to her, "The Holy Spirit will come upon you, and the power of the Highest will overshadow you; therefore, also, that Holy One who is to be born will be called the Son of God." - Luke 1:26-35*

These verses tell us a lot about the character of Mary, the woman chosen by God to be the mother of Jesus. Verse 27 reveals that she was a virgin betrothed to Joseph of the house of David. So, she was chaste . . . engaged to be married, but still a virgin. Verse 38 shows that she was obedient. When informed by the angel Gabriel that she was to bear the Son of God, she answered: "Behold the maidservant of the Lord! Let it be to me according to your word."

In this we see that Mary was full of faith and was quick to submit to God's will. Her humility is apparent by her words recorded in verse 48: "For He has regarded the lowly state of His maidservant; For behold, henceforth all generations will call me blessed."

We learn from this the kind of woman God chooses to fulfill His purpose: chaste, obedient, humble, and full of faith.

God chose a young woman of strong character to be the mother of Jesus. Mary quietly accepted a situation that she knew would cause controversy. She was willing to risk being accused of breaking her marriage contract by adultery. This would surely bring scorn and the wrath of the people upon her. Mary didn't claim to understand what was about to happen to her. She simply worshipped God, saying: "My soul magnifies the Lord (Luke 1:46). Her humble obedience made her a party in the miracle of the Incarnation at a level no other human can perceive. Her example has certainly resulted in all generations since calling her blessed.

Almighty God chose Joseph to be the human surrogate father of the Son of God. What an honor this was for him.

His reaction and response to the situation he was put in reveals something about his character. Listen to the account in Matthew 1:18–25:

> *Now the birth of Jesus Christ was as follows: After His mother Mary was betrothed to Joseph, before they came together, she was found with child of the Holy Spirit. Then Joseph her husband, being a just man, and not wanting to make her a public example, was minded to put her away secretly. But while he thought about these things, behold, an angel of the Lord appeared to him in a dream, saying, "Joseph, son of David, do not be afraid to take to you Mary your wife, for that which is conceived in her is of the Holy Spirit. And she will bring forth a Son, and you shall call His name JESUS, for He will save His people from their sins."*

Chapter 22

> *So all this was done that it might be fulfilled which was spoken by the Lord through the prophet, saying: "Behold, the virgin shall be with child, and bear a Son, and they shall call His name Immanuel" which is translated, "God with us." Then Joseph, being aroused from sleep, did as the angel of the Lord commanded him and took to him his wife, and did not know her till she had brought forth her firstborn Son. And he called His name JESUS.*

Joseph showed himself to be pious, kind, charitable, obedient and chaste. He is a great example of the kind of man God chooses to fulfill His purposes.

The Provision of Protection

Protection from Herod

Our Heavenly Father in His great love for His Son, made sure that no harm would come to Him. He knew that wicked King Herod would be out to get Him.

How evil was Herod the Great? He had the nasty habit of killing anyone he suspected of plotting to take over his ill-gotten throne. He even knocked off one of his ten wives and three of his sons. What a guy! He heard that the baby Jesus would be the King of the Jews, so naturally, he saw him as a threat.

> *Then Herod, when he had secretly called the wise men, determined from them what time the star appeared. And he sent them to Bethlehem and said, "Go and search carefully for the young Child, and when you have found Him, bring back word to me, that I may come and worship Him also." When they heard the king, they departed; and behold, the star which they had seen*

> *in the East went before them, till it came and stood over where the young Child was. When they saw the star, they rejoiced with exceedingly great joy. And when they had come into the house, they saw the young Child with Mary His mother, and fell down and worshiped Him. And when they had opened their treasures, they presented gifts to Him: gold, frankincense, and myrrh. - Matt. 2:7–11*

To protect His Son, Father God sent an angel with a warning to the baby Jesus's stepfather.

> *Then, being divinely warned in a dream that they should not return to Herod, they departed for their own country another way. Now when they had departed, behold, an angel of the Lord appeared to Joseph in a dream, saying, "Arise, take the young Child and His mother, flee to Egypt, and stay there until I bring you word; for Herod will seek the young Child to destroy Him." When he arose, he took the young Child and His mother by night and departed for Egypt, and was there until the death of Herod, that it might be fulfilled which was spoken by the Lord through the prophet, saying, "Out of Egypt I called My Son." Then Herod, when he saw that he was deceived by the wise men, was exceedingly angry; and he sent forth and put to death all the male children who were in Bethlehem and in all its districts, from two years old and under, according to the time which he had determined from the wise men. - Matt. 2:12–16*

Jesus was blessed to have both divine Father Love and human Father Love protecting Him and His mother Mary. Don't all children need both?

Chapter 22

The Provision of Resources

God chose well for Jesus' family

In the telling of the Christmas Story, Mary and Joseph are often portrayed as poor and homeless. They were neither.

Joseph's carpentry business probably did very well. Besides, both mother and stepfather were royalty—from the line of King David. That doesn't necessarily mean they were wealthy, but there is a possibility of it.

"But didn't they have to find shelter in a stable?" you ask. Indeed they did. Bethlehem was crowded. They had been sleeping under the stars while traveling. So, a room in an inn would have been nice, but it wasn't a five-star hotel. Far from it! No running water, flushing toilets, or air conditioning. Besides, there was no way to have made a reservation, seeing that telephones and the Internet hadn't been invented. So, they slept with the animals. I jest, but at least they had shelter.

It could be that the Bible's reference to swaddling clothes causes some to think Mary wrapped the baby Jesus in rags. They were not rags. Swaddling *cloths* are strips of fabric that are used to tightly wrap newborns to keep them warm and to provide them with a sense of comfort, as in the womb.

Perhaps the line "I am a poor boy, too" in "The Little Drummer Boy" song has contributed to the notion that Jesus's family was poor. Jehovah Jireh, our provider, made sure that His Son's human family had the resources necessary to well care for His Son while the King of Kings was growing up.

To further ensure that there would be no financial need unmet, the Father dispatched wise men from the East to bring expensive treasures. We don't know how many there were. The Bible doesn't say. Again, a Christmas song numbers them "Three Wise Men," but for all we know, there could have been twelve. What we do know is that there were three forms of riches.

> *And when they had come into the house, they saw the young Child with Mary His mother, and fell down and worshiped Him. And when they had opened their treasures, they presented gifts to Him: gold, frankincense, and myrrh. - Matt. 2:11*

By this time—up to two years after Jesus's birth—they were living in a house, perhaps built by Joseph, purchased or rented. Either way, it is unlikely that a poor, homeless family could have achieved that in less than two years.

God chose well when he selected Joseph to be the surrogate father to His Son. And of course, Mary the mother of Jesus was "...blessed . . . among women" (Luke 1:42). It should not be surprising that God's Father Love makes Him a great provider.

Chapter 22

Stay-Home Father Love—Bill's Story

Bill had a high-paying, upwardly mobile job at a major corporation, and his wife's professional career was thriving as well. But the birth of their third child and other extenuating circumstances brought on a difficult childcare dilemma: Who was going to stay home with her and their other two children?

Normally, in America, the decision is a no-brainer. It's usually the mom who stays at home. But that didn't make the best sense to Bill and his wife. So, they decided that Bill would become a stay-home dad, a decision that has blossomed for him into a successful career in politics that has led him to the state senate.

"It was an acceptance of what's important, and a decision that was prayed on," Bill said. "Clearly, for me, this was an opportunity to help raise my children, something a lot of dads don't have. We based this on what was best for the family, what was best for the children."

That was 1999, and as you might imagine, society wasn't very welcoming. "It was a novel decision," Bill admitted. "I knew of one other at-home dad at the time. And it was a novelty among the other moms. Some moms don't want the guys around. Some public opinion was against me," he continued. "As a white male, it is the closest I came to discrimination. They were judging me because of how I chose to live my life."

Bill filled that role full-time for several years. He even helped start a stay-home dads' group in his area, first web-only and then later developing into meetings and events. Then, as the years passed, it evolved into something more. Bill got involved in his community, served on his city council, and has become a state senator.

"I would argue that becoming a stay-at-home dad made me a public servant," he said. "It is why I got involved in my community and started serving it. I gained a hyper-awareness of the value of child-rearing by having 'hands on' experience. It helped shape my thinking on many issues, like early childhood education. I never thought of it like that as I was doing it."

Bill gained personally as well. "My benefit is a couple of things," he said. "I enjoy a relationship with my children that a lot of fathers would envy. A lot of fathers have bonds with their children, but I think I have a bond with mine that is special.

"And then there's my career. To step off a cliff and walk away from a good-paying job with retirement and health insurance was terrifying," he continued. "I almost didn't do it. But we took the leap of faith and have been rewarded many times for it."

However, what about the children? Remember, this decision was made at the time with their best interests in mind. "I think our kids have benefited from having a rich relationship with both parents," he said. "The maternal bond is a rich experience, and they definitely didn't miss out on that. But I think they have grown up looking at things a little differently. They benefited from that balance."

Chapter 22

CHAPTER 23
A Father's Spiritual Toolbox

Christian fathers are instructed to raise their children to become responsible adults. To accomplish this, we must deal with our children in love.

Some Responsibilities of Fathering

Love God and Diligently Teach Children His Commandments

> Hear, O Israel: The LORD our God, the LORD **is** one! You shall love the LORD your God with all your heart, with all your soul, and with all your strength. And these words which I command you today shall be in your heart. You shall teach them diligently to your children, and shall talk of them when you sit in your house, when you walk by the way, when you lie down, and when you rise up. You shall bind them as a sign on your hand, and they shall be as frontlets between your eyes. Deut. 6:4–8

> Only take heed to yourself, and diligently keep yourself, lest you forget the things your eyes have seen, and lest they depart from your heart all the days of your life. And teach them to your children and your grandchildren. - Deut. 4:9

We cannot depend upon our child's school teachers, Sunday school teachers, or youth program leaders for this. It is our job, along with our child's mother, primarily to be our children's teachers of God's ways.

Train Your Children

Bible instruction is: "Train up a child in the way he should go, And when he is old he will not depart from it (Prov. 22:6)." Of course, our children should go in the direction of the Lord. As their spiritual leader, it is our responsibility to lead them that way, both by example and teaching. It is also our job as parents to ask God to show us how our child is wired; what his gifts and talents are; what her likes and dislikes are; what God's plans for him are. Then we must seek God's guidance on how to direct the child in the way they should go. This wise, God-directed training will stay with a child for life.

Provide for Your Children

It is a father's God-ordained responsibility to be the primary breadwinner for the family. The Word says plainly: "But if anyone does not provide for his own, and especially for those of his household, he has denied the faith and is worse than an unbeliever (1 Tim. 5:8)."

A father's responsibility is to take the lead in providing not only financially, but also spiritually, emotionally, academically, recreationally, etc. for his family. It's a big job, but with God's help we can do it well.

CHAPTER 24
My Dream

"I have a dream that my four little children will one day live in a nation where they will not be judged by the color of their skin but by the content of their character." – Dr Martin Luther King, Jr.[lxviii]

Surely, Dr. King would be heartbroken—as am I—that our culture, more than a half century after the "I Have a Dream" speech, is not producing more men and women of character. And our children are paying a high price.

Nearly two out of three African American children will go to bed tonight in a home where their biological father does not live.[lxix] That's a real catastrophe.

Poverty, crime, school failure, drug trafficking, and murder *thrive* in neighborhoods where responsible fathers are missing. In such neighborhoods, people live in fear. They are even too afraid to testify against those who are perpetrating the crimes. We are in desperate need of more protectors, order keepers, providers, and stabilizers.

More than five decades after Martin Luther King's dream, educated African American men and women are lamenting that they can't find suitable mates. That's *not* what Dr. King dreamed for us. It is, in fact, a nightmare!

But, I too have a dream!

Chapter 24

My dream is rooted in my personal experience of having known many good men. I have a dream today. It's a dream that gives me hope, despite the crisis of father absence plaguing our nation, and the sad state of so many black males.

I'm dreaming of a time when men are sufficiently men . . . who stand up and say: "Enough is enough! You can't have my neighborhood. You can't sell those drugs here. You can't smoke that here. You can't rob that store. You can't jack that car. You can't shoot that gun. This is *my* neighborhood. This is *my* city. These are *my* children . . . all of these children. These are *my* seniors . . . all of these seniors. And you can't hurt them. I'm a man. And I am a POPS!" That's Father Love.

I dream of a day when healthy manhood and responsible fatherhood are restored in America, when good men are celebrated for the God-given role they fill in society. I dream of a time when fathers are honored rather than portrayed as bumbling idiots on TV and in movies.

I dream of a day when *every* father is man enough to raise his children well, when all men strive to overcome every barrier that keeps them separated from their kids—and make no mistake, some barriers are mighty. I dream of a time when society understands and appreciates the importance of fathers in the lives of their children and works to remove every impediment to their role.

In my dream, every father is man enough to change diapers, help with homework, visit the school, go to their kids' games and plays, where we are men enough to be present, whether we can *give* presents. I dream of a time when mothers support their children's fathers in their co-parenting. In my dream, every father watches with pride in their heart as their children receive their diplomas and degrees with honors.

I dream of a great day when all young men have the character to resist the urge to follow the crowd into boyish behavior. My dream is to see a day when they are brave enough to stand up for what is right, even when what is wrong is more popular. That will be a day when family, church, school, and work keep young men grounded.

On that day, men are guardians of their families, their neighborhood, their city, and all that is precious. With the power of Father Love, they will do this.

That's what I am dreaming. Are you dreaming with me?

I dream of a day when systems stop treating fathers like second-class parents. In that day, non-custodial fathers, too, have legal rights when it comes to their kids. We will stop calling it "visitation" and start calling it "parenting time."

On that blessed day, we will recognize that not all fathers who have child support arrearages are deadbeat . . . some are just dead broke and beat down.

Someday, all women will know that fathers cannot be replaced. Social agencies and governments will understand that programs — no matter how good — cannot be mommies and daddies. They'll know that it takes a man to be a father, and that it takes Father Love to be a great POPS.

That'll be a day when unemployed dads are valued for what they can contribute to their children's well-being, when even

Chapter 24

incarcerated fathers know that they have something good they can give their kids . . . their letters, phone, and video calls.

I dream of a day when men are mature enough to embrace commitment rather than avoid it. Then, all men will love their women enough to marry them. That's when all men are men enough to commit to their women for life . . . for better, for worse, for richer, for poorer, in sickness and in health, to love and to cherish. In *that* day, women will know that "*Maybe* I do" won't do.

That will be the day when every little girl's first boyfriend will be her daddy, and her daddy shows his little princess what it means to be loved and respected. His tender affections will raise the bar so high that she won't settle for any less of a man when the time comes for her to choose a mate. That will be a time when boys see their loving mother in every girl, when domestic violence is a thing of the past.

Yes, I too have a dream.

I'm dreaming of the day when every child has both a mother and a father working together for the benefit of their child, whether they like each other or not.

I dream of a day when every little boy has a hero at home to look up to. I see a hero who may not rap, slam dunk, run touchdowns, or hit home runs, but who is man enough to love his children with all his heart. I envision men who prove it by giving their children lots of their time. This man will be a hero who does his best to show his sons and daughters the right way to go. That's what I'm dreaming. Are you dreaming with me?

But this is more than I dream I dream. It's a vision. And it's a necessity. We *must* turn this dream into a mission of heartfelt prayer and hard work. We *must* help our boys become men. And they *must* become men who see themselves the way God created them to be . . . *real* men who are providers and protectors, heroes and husbands. That day, they will be men who strive to love the way God does.

We *must* help our young males develop into genuine men . . . and we *must* support fathers as they strive to become responsible parents. This is not about fathers over mothers. It is about recognizing that children need both. We must do these things for the sake of our children, our families, our neighborhoods, our city, our country, our legacy as a society. We *must* make this vision a reality.

It's not too late to change things. But we first must acknowledge that the great social experiment of the 1960s — "anything goes," "love the one you're with," "sex, drugs, and rock and roll," and "lookin' out for No. 1" — has failed miserably. It's time to get back to building families and raising kids God's way.

And when we do this with God's enablement, we will be the ones — as the prophet Isaiah foretold — who will "rebuild the deserted ruins of [our] cities. Then [we] will be known as a rebuilder of walls and a restorer of homes." (Isaiah 58:12 NLT)

When we make this dream a reality, we will be the generation that reclaims our destiny, the ones who rebuild the family, the people who save our nation.

Thank God for Dr. King, who showed us the power of a dream. Let's celebrate him today. But let us not stop dreaming dreams. I believe we honor him and our Lord when we keep dreaming new dreams for a better world. There is much to be done, and there is a short time to do it. Together, let us envision a new America where

Chapter 24

every child has the security of a strong and healthy family, with a dad who excels in Father Love.

CHAPTER 25
What You and Your Community Can Do

The father-absence crisis can be effectively addressed when communities commit to it. It starts with leadership. We don't know how the prophets Elijah and John did it, but Scripture says that they turned "the hearts of fathers to their children." (See Mal. 4:6 and Luke 1:17 NKJV)

A father's heart that is filled with love for his children is a powerful resource for them. That love can and should be nurtured in fathers. Since 2006, the Urban Light Ministries,[lxx] team of fatherhood practitioners have employed the well-regarded Nurturing Fathers Program[lxxi] to help men develop skills and attitudes for male nurturance. Since then, we have developed our own introduction to healthy fathering principles and practices called POPS 101. It is a four-session course, available in person and online in English and Spanish.[lxxii] Since publishing the first edition of this book, I have developed the Father Love Study Guide and a thirteen-session Father Love program that covers the content of this book.[lxxiii]

Recently, a member of our team, Bruce Stapleton, published the book Fathering Strong: God's Blueprint for Leading Your Family.[lxxiv] There is an accompanying devotional, study guide, and a facilitator's guide. This adds to Urban Light Ministries' suite of resources that includes the weekly Fathering Strong Podcast[lxxv], the Fathering Strong Blog[lxxvi], and the Fathering Strong App, which we developed to provide a private online and mobile platform for fathers to build community and to encourage one another in their parenting journey.[lxxvii]

Another effective program for fathers we have utilized is On My Shoulders,[lxxviii] a course to help men acquire tools for building healthy relationships with their children and their children's mothers. We've worked with dozens of groups of men in various locations, including our center, county jails, prisons, drug treatment centers, and churches. Hundreds of fathers throughout the Miami Valley of Ohio and beyond have been helped to be better dads through these programs.

Other excellent fatherhood curricula, though not Bible-based, is offered by the National Fatherhood Initiative,[lxxix] COPES (Council on Prevention and Education: Substances),[lxxx] and others.

Beyond fatherhood classes, and the other helpful resources, many fathers need additional, long-term support to achieve stability for the sake of their children and families. Meeting their many needs can be expensive, but father absence is a lot more costly.

The Challenge

As I mentioned earlier, the annual cost of father absence in America is staggering. In 2006, the Federal Government spent at least **$99.8 billion** providing assistance to father-absent homes. This figure, derived from a study by Nock and Einolf (2008), was a conservative estimate, intentionally excluding federal benefit programs for entire communities, indirect costs related to the poorer outcomes of children from father-absent homes, and long-term costs such as reduced tax income from lower-earning, single-parent families.

What You and Your Community Can Do

While a precise updated federal expenditure figure for assistance to father-absent homes is not routinely compiled, research consistently indicates that the economic and social costs associated with father absence remain substantial and place a considerable burden on taxpayers. These costs stem from increased reliance on various social safety net programs and the broader societal impacts of negative outcomes often linked to fatherlessness, such as higher rates of poverty, increased incarceration, and poorer educational attainment. Experts continue to highlight these indirect and long-term costs as significant, making the true financial impact much higher than direct assistance figures alone suggest.

The cost to individual states is also significant. A 2022 report from the Mississippi Office of the State Auditor estimated that fatherlessness costs Mississippi taxpayers over **$700 million** each year due to increased incarceration rates, education costs, and other factors. While this is just one state, and a small one at that, it provides a sense of the scale of the financial burden of fatherlessness. Very conservatively multiplying that number by 50 produces a mind blowing **$35 trillion** per year! The actual number is likely much higher.

This is a disaster on every level! Everyone is impacted. Every person, every business in every sector, is paying a high price for father absence. There is a clear connection between father absence and teen pregnancy, since a father's behavior and values uniquely influence a girl's expectations about boyfriends and husbands. In addition, boys learn from their fathers what kind of husband and father they should become and how to treat girls and women. Research shows that boys raised in single-mother homes are at a higher risk of teen pregnancy and teenage girls without fathers were twice as likely to be involved in early sexual activity and seven times more likely to get pregnant as other adolescents.

Chapter 25

Father involvement plays an important role in reducing drug and alcohol use among youth. Researchers at Columbia University found that children living in two-parent households with a poor relationship with their father are 68 percent more likely to smoke, drink, or use drugs compared to all teens in two-parent households. Moreover, teens in single-mother households fared much worse. They had a 30 percent higher risk than those in all two-parent households.

Children who grow up without their fathers are at greatest risk for child abuse. In fact, the presence of a child's father in the home lowers the likelihood that a child will be abused. Compared to living with both parents, living in a single-parent home doubles the risk that a child will suffer physical, emotional, or educational neglect.[lxxxi]

Champions are Needed

When community leadership is made aware of the calamitous local situation for children and how it impacts them, they can then be enlisted as champions of the cause. It takes a persistent, sustained effort to transform a fatherless culture. But it begins one heart at a time.

A community mobilization effort can be started with a small investment. Most communities fail to seriously and persistently address the father absence and related family fragmentation issues due to lack of leadership. Don't let that happen in your community! The budget should include dollars for the lead person's salary and for special events. Possible sources of funding are local foundations, United Way, county governments, and local businesses.

Required community connections and non-financial resources include partnerships with county social services agencies, local elected officials, school districts, local colleges, fatherhood program agencies, clergy leaders, faith-based agencies, and others. Leadership summits are useful for raising awareness among leaders in each sector.

Do the Research

Using the latest census data for your community, determine the extent of fatherlessness. Your county's public health department may already have done this research. If not, that's a good place to begin making inquiries. A local university may also be a good resource for this data.

Identify the Gaps

Conduct a survey of the existing father-specific direct service programs in your community. Interview local fathers to determine their top needs and the most common barriers they face. Compare the top needs with the existing services and resources for dads. Lead the team to agreement on the top three unmet needs.

Respond to the Needs of Fathers

Let's say that your leadership team forms a consensus that low-income, non-resident fathers of young children should be targeted first. Rally the team to initiate a project to address one of the top needs of those fathers. Make it a collaborative effort between several organizations. Seek programming support from a variety of community agencies. Seek to be holistic in your approach, giving due consideration to the financial, educational, emotional, spiritual, housing, transportation, and other needs of the participants. Remember, the healthier and more stable the father, the more powerful the resource he can be for his children.

The Challenge of Sustainability

Maintaining a fatherhood community mobilization effort is a daunting task. It is a national challenge. There has long been a need for reliable sources of funding and other resources specifically for responsible fatherhood work. Despite the clear need to enhance the well-being of children by increasing the number of responsible and skilled fathers, funding for that important work has been tenuous at best.

A 2012 report by the Center for Research on Fathers, Children, and Family Well-Being at Columbia University stated: "Thirteen years have passed since the last comprehensive *review of the fatherhood field. In the interim, two recessions, funding cuts, and tight fiscal conditions have made it extremely unlikely that states would fund fatherhood initiatives without federal subsidies. Given diminished opportunities to leverage public funds for responsible fatherhood, organized philanthropy has also reduced funding for responsible fatherhood. As a result of changing funding requirements, rapidly evolving program priorities, and increasing demands for evidence-based practice, the field of responsible fatherhood has, in some sense, lost its center of gravity. It has been tossed on a sea of change."[lxxxii]

In 2025, the sentiment from the 2012 report remains largely accurate; **federal subsidies** are still the primary funding source for most large-scale fatherhood initiatives in the United States. While the fiscal climate has changed since 2012, state funding for these programs continues to be inconsistent and often insufficient without federal support.

Federal Funding

The main source of federal funding continues to be the **Healthy Marriage and Responsible Fatherhood (HMRF)** grant program. Congress has reauthorized this program multiple times since 2012, with the most recent funding cycle awarding grants in 2020. This indicates a continued commitment from the federal government to subsidize programs that focus on strengthening relationships and promoting father engagement. These federal grants allow states and local organizations to provide services like parenting education, job training, and conflict resolution, which would be difficult to fund otherwise.

State-Level Initiatives

While many states still rely heavily on federal HMRF grants, a few have initiated or increased their own funding for fatherhood programs. The increased recognition of the economic and social costs of **father absence** has prompted some state-level action.

Both Florida and Ohio have recently made significant legislative and financial commitments to supporting fatherhood initiatives, with a focus on strengthening families and addressing the societal costs of father absence.

Florida

In 2022, Florida's Governor Ron DeSantis signed HB 7065 into law, creating the **Responsible Fatherhood Initiative**. This historic legislation appropriated over **$68.9 million** to fund a number of programs and services. The initiative is designed to highlight the critical role of fathers and provides a wide range of support, including:

- **Grants for Non-profits:** Funding for community-based non-profit organizations that offer services to address the comprehensive needs of fathers, such as employment assistance, child support management, and parenting skills.

- **Mentorship Programs:** Support for mentorship programs aimed at at-risk male students in middle and high school.

- **Public Awareness Campaign:** A statewide campaign to promote responsible fatherhood and provide resources to fathers.

- **Father Engagement Specialists:** The legislation also requires community-based care agencies to hire father engagement specialists to increase father involvement in programs.

Ohio

Ohio has also recently made a major investment in its fatherhood programs. The state's new budget includes a **$20 million** investment in the **Responsible Fatherhood Initiative**, which will be overseen by the existing **Ohio Commission on Fatherhood**. This funding is in addition to the commission's regular budget. Key aspects of Ohio's recent efforts include:

- **Dedicated Funding:** The significant allocation of funds demonstrates a legislative priority to address fatherlessness, which is cited by supporters as a factor in community poverty, crime, and child behavioral problems.

What You and Your Community Can Do

- **Grant Administration:** The new funds will be administered to organizations with a track record of effective fatherhood programs.

- **Modeling Florida:** Ohio's initiative has been publicly stated to be modeled after Florida's successful program, with leaders from both states collaborating to promote the importance of fatherhood.

- **Long-Standing Commission:** Ohio is unique in that it has had a legislatively authorized and funded fatherhood commission since 2000, and this recent funding is a major expansion of its work.

Other states, like Mississippi, have begun to quantify the high cost of father absence to taxpayers, providing a financial incentive for state-funded programs. This shift, however, is not widespread, and the overall landscape remains heavily dependent on federal subsidies to sustain these critical services.

Needed: More Workers in the Field

Anyone can be a champion for fatherhood. There are practical ways you can help. Begin right at home and with your own family. Reach out to others in your community. Mentor a fatherless youngster. Speak out against bad behavior. Advocate for parents and families. Coach a young father.

It begins with acknowledging that children truly need the powerful resource of Father Love, and then taking whatever action you can to support dads as they strive to love their kids with all their hearts.

Chapter 25

Another problem is the inability of local service providers, with notable exceptions, to attract private funding to pay for responsible fatherhood work. Fortunately, there are non-profit organizations that are already working with fathers and families, but they're struggling due to the reliance upon a relatively small amount of government funding. What a shame that the very folks—heroes in my mind—who are out there addressing this massive crisis, working with fathers to help them be better parents, are besieged by a constant lack of reliable funding. This must change.

CHAPTER 26
What Christian Churches Can and Must Do

In my view, no entity is better positioned to effectively address the fatherhood crisis than the global Christian Church. Who else can raise an army of fathers to be godly servant leaders in their homes and mentors of men and fatherless boys in their communities? In the process, men become better husbands, children are nurtured, and congregations grow spiritually, numerically, and financially. What could be greater outcomes?

The Christian Church has a clear biblical mandate to address the father absence crisis in its congregations and local communities; a calling rooted in several core scriptural themes. First and foremost, the Bible repeatedly commands believers to care for the "fatherless and the orphan," a directive found in passages like James 1:27. This is understood as a call for the Church, as the body of Christ, to act as a support system for vulnerable children and families affected by absent fathers. Furthermore, the concept of God as the ultimate Father is central to the Christian faith.

With God described as "a father to the fatherless" in Psalm 68:5, the Church is tasked with modeling this divine fatherhood and helping children understand God's love, especially when they lack a positive human example. This responsibility extends to the biblical emphasis on discipleship and mentoring.

Chapter 26

The Church is called to raise up Christian men who can not only be good fathers themselves but also mentor younger men and boys who may be growing up without a father figure, helping to "turn the hearts of the fathers to their children," as prophesied in Malachi 4:6.

Finally, the Bible's focus on the importance of strong families as the foundation of society compels the Church to support and strengthen families, investing in fathers to build up both their own households and the wider community. In essence, the Church's mandate is a holistic one: to directly support those in need, to mentor and equip men, and to uphold the value of biblical fatherhood as a reflection of God's character.

We are seeking to inspire a new movement of churches that are committed to developing fatherhood ministries within their churches to raise up men who are spiritual leaders of their families, servant-leaders in their congregations, and inspirational examples in their communities.

A Vision for Building Strong Fathers: Comprehensive Church-Based Fatherhood Ministry

The modern church faces an unprecedented opportunity to address one of society's most pressing challenges: the fatherhood crisis. As communities grapple with the far-reaching effects of father absence and disengagement, the church stands uniquely positioned to provide biblical solutions that transform not only individual men but entire families and communities. A comprehensive church-based fatherhood ministry represents far more than a program or occasional event; it embodies a strategic

What Christian Churches Can and Must Do

discipleship initiative that recognizes fathers as the spiritual servant leaders of their homes and in their communities.

The ripple effect of effective Comprehensive Church-Based Fatherhood Ministry extends far beyond the church walls. When fathers are biblically grounded, relationally connected, and practically equipped, they become catalysts for transformation that impacts their marriages, children, extended families, and broader community networks. Strong fathers contribute to strong families, which in turn build solid congregations that serve as pillars of healthy communities. This positive cycle creates safer neighborhoods, more effective schools, reduced crime rates, and increased prosperity for all residents.

At its core, Comprehensive Church-Based Fatherhood Ministry answers Jesus' call for His followers to be the salt and light of the world.

> *13 "You are the salt of the earth; but if the salt loses its flavor, how shall it be seasoned? It is then good for nothing but to be thrown out and trampled underfoot by men.*
>
> *14 "You are the light of the world. A city that is set on a hill cannot be hidden. 15 Nor do they light a lamp and put it under a basket, but on a lampstand, and it gives light to all who are in the house. 16 Let your light so shine before men, that they may see your good works and glorify your Father in heaven. – Matthew 5:13-16*

Salt preserves, flavors, and purifies, while light illuminates truth, provides guidance, and dispels darkness. Fathers who embrace their biblical calling serve these exact functions within their families and communities, standing against moral decay, bringing distinctive Christian character to their relationships, and guiding their children in the ways of the Lord.

It is our Lord's Great Commission for the Church to preach the Gospel of Jesus Christ and to make disciples for Him who are salt and light in their homes, churches, and communities.[lxxxiii]

Program Overview: The Fathering Strong Ministry Model

The Fathering Strong Comprehensive Church-Based Fatherhood Ministry model represents a comprehensive approach to church-based fatherhood ministry that integrates biblical foundations with practical application. This model recognizes that effective fatherhood ministry must address the whole man, encompassing his spiritual development, relational skills, practical parenting abilities, and personal well-being. Comprehensive Church-Based Fatherhood Ministry operates on the principle that fathers are not merely recipients of ministry but active participants in their own growth and the development of other men.

The Comprehensive Church-Based Fatherhood Ministry model is built upon five foundational pillars that work synergistically to create lasting transformation. These pillars include establishing biblical foundations, engaging fathers relationally, equipping them with practical skills and resources, empowering them for leadership and service, and creating sustainable community connections that provide ongoing support and accountability.

Comprehensive Church-Based Fatherhood Ministry recognizes that fathers come to the ministry at different stages of their journey. Some are expectant fathers preparing for their first child, while others are seasoned parents seeking to improve their effectiveness. Some men are married and living with their children, while others are divorced, separated, or never-married fathers working to maintain meaningful relationships with their children. Still others have made significant mistakes, are suffering the consequences of damaged relationships, and are trying to do better. The ministry model accommodates this diversity through flexible programming that meets men where they are while challenging them to grow toward biblical maturity.

Central to Comprehensive Church-Based Fatherhood Ministry's effectiveness is its integration with the church's broader discipleship strategy. Rather than operating as an isolated ministry, fatherhood development is woven throughout the church's teaching, small group structure, men's ministry, and family programming. This integration ensures that fathers receive consistent messages about their calling and have multiple touchpoints for growth and support.

Foundational Principles

The theological foundation of Comprehensive Church-Based Fatherhood Ministry rests upon the biblical understanding of fatherhood as a sacred calling that reflects God's own character as Father. Scripture presents fathers as spiritual leaders, protectors, providers, and nurturers who are responsible for the physical, emotional, and spiritual development of their children. This calling extends beyond biological fathers to include stepfathers, adoptive fathers, and spiritual fathers who invest in the lives of children and younger men.

Comprehensive Church-Based Fatherhood Ministry embraces a gospel-centered approach that acknowledges the reality of human brokenness while proclaiming the transformative power of God's grace. Many men enter fatherhood carrying wounds from their own childhood experiences, struggling with feelings of inadequacy, or battling destructive patterns learned from previous generations. The gospel message offers hope for healing, forgiveness for past failures, and power for future transformation. This grace-based approach creates a safe environment where men can be honest about their struggles while receiving encouragement and practical help for growth.

Discipleship forms the core methodology of Comprehensive Church-Based Fatherhood Ministry, recognizing that effective fatherhood flows from spiritual maturity and character development. The program views fatherhood as both a context for discipleship and a result of discipleship. As men grow in their relationship with Christ, they naturally become better fathers. However, they "don't know what they don't know"[lxxxiv] about fathering. Simultaneously, the challenges and responsibilities of fatherhood drive men toward deeper dependence on God and greater commitment to spiritual growth.

Comprehensive Church-Based Fatherhood Ministry adopts a holistic approach that addresses all dimensions of a man's life. While spiritual development remains central, the program also provides practical training in parenting skills, marriage enrichment, financial stewardship, emotional intelligence, and physical health. This comprehensive approach recognizes that fathers cannot compartmentalize their lives; effectiveness in one area impacts all other areas.

Community and accountability serve as essential elements that distinguish Comprehensive Church-Based Fatherhood Ministry from individualistic approaches to personal development. Comprehensive Church-Based Fatherhood Ministry creates multiple opportunities for men to build meaningful relationships with other fathers, share their experiences, learn from one another, and provide mutual support and encouragement. These relationships often extend beyond the formal program structure, creating lasting friendships that provide ongoing accountability and support.

Program Structure and Components

Comprehensive Church-Based Fatherhood Ministry begins with a foundation-building phase designed to establish biblical understanding, build relationships among participants, and assess individual needs and goals. The program structure is built in phases:

- Phase One: Foundation Building
- Phase Two: Skill Development
- Phase Three: Leadership Development

Comprehensive Church-Based Fatherhood Ministry provides continued support and accountability for program graduates through building and maintaining community among the participants through:

- Small Groups
- Mentoring Program
- Online, Digital and Mobile Resources

Special programs and events could include:

- Father-Child Activities
- Annual Signature Events
- Seasonal Celebrations

Recognizing that strong marriages provide the foundation for effective fatherhood, Comprehensive Church-Based Fatherhood Ministry includes regular marriage enrichment opportunities such as.

- Date night events
- Marriage retreats
- Ongoing marriage small groups

Community Outreach

As salt and light influence what they encounter, the outgrowth of spiritual leadership in the home and community should be impactful for Christ in the community. Comprehensive Church-Based Fatherhood Ministry extends its impact beyond the church walls through various community outreach initiatives that demonstrate the love of Christ while addressing practical needs in the broader community. These programs provide opportunities for fathers to model Christian service and compassion for their children while making a positive difference in their communities. All of this, while prioritizing family and church responsibilities. These opportunities can include:

- School Partnerships
- Youth Sports Coaching and Officiating
- Community Service Projects

Crisis Support

Comprehensive Church-Based Fatherhood Ministry recognizes that fathers face various crises that can threaten their effectiveness and well-being. A crisis support system provides immediate assistance and ongoing support for fathers dealing with job loss, divorce, serious illness, death of family members, or other traumatic experiences. This support can include:

- Emergency Assistance
- Specialized Support Groups
- Professional Referral Networks

I am excited about continuing the development of the Comprehensive Church-Based Fatherhood Ministry framework along with a couple of beta churches. These pastors are committed to "turning the hearts of fathers to their children," [lxxxv] while helping their men be better husbands, parents, church members, and community servant leaders. Together, we are believing God for congregational growth spiritually, numerically, and financially.

If you are interested in your church joining the mission to increase the father love in your community through Comprehensive Church-Based Fatherhood Ministry, please reach out to me personally for a conversation.

Eli Williams, Consultant/Coach

Email: eli@pastoreli.com

Phone: (937) 408-1050

Urban Light Ministries Incorporated

Email: info@urbanlight.org

Web: www.urbanlight.org

Phone: (937) 727-4891

Mail: P.O. Box 3132 | Springfield, Ohio 45501

REFERENCES

[i] www.urbanlight.org

[ii] https://urbanlight.org/fathering-strong/

[iii] https://www.youtube.com/watch?v=q6uyEJNmRRY

[iv] www.todaysnewhope.org

[v] While the original source cited 2011 data, more recent statistics from the U.S. Census Bureau consistently show this disparity. For example, explore tables related to poverty status of families by type of family and presence of children under 18. A good starting point would be data from the American Community Survey (ACS) or Current Population Survey (CPS) from the U.S. Census Bureau. For example, "Income and Poverty in the United States" reports annually include these breakdowns.

[vi] This remains a consistent finding across various studies. General support for this statement can be found in publications from the U.S. Department of Health and Human Services, Substance Abuse and Mental Health Services Administration (SAMHSA), and academic research on adolescent development and family structure.

[vii] This continues to be supported by sociological and public health research. For ongoing research in this area, look for studies

References

published in journals such as *Journal of Marriage and Family*, *Journal of Health and Social Behavior*, or those linked to organizations like the National Institute on Drug Abuse (NIDA).

[viii] This finding is well-established in child development and family studies. For current research, consult journals like *Demography*, *Journal of Family Psychology*, or *Child Development*, which frequently publish studies on family structure and child outcomes.

[ix] Updated statistics on children's living arrangements are regularly released by the U.S. Census Bureau. Specifically, look for data under "Families and Households" or "Children's Characteristics." For example, reports like "Children's Living Arrangements and Characteristics" (if still published in that format) or the data explorer tools on the Census Bureau website.

[x] The economic impact of father absence is a topic of ongoing discussion and analysis. While the specific 2006 GAO study is now dated, organizations like the Annie E. Casey Foundation, think tanks focusing on family policy, and academic researchers continue to quantify the societal costs associated with single-parent households and related social challenges. Searching for "cost of father absence" or "economic impact of family structure" can lead to more recent estimates and analyses.

[xi] Read John 3:16-17

[xii] Galatians 5:22

[xiii] Gal. 5:22

xiv Benjamin Franklin (1706–1790). Poor Richard's Almanack, February 1755

xv Rom. 2:4

xvi Galatians 5:22

xvii Col. 3:12–14

xviii Col. 3:8

xix Col. 3:18–21

xx See Romans 12:15

xxi Matthew Henry's Exposition of the Old and New Testaments, also known as his Complete Commentary on the Whole Bible. Specifically, the quote appears in his commentary on the New Testament, in the section for 1 Corinthians 8.

xxii 2 Chronicles 7:14

xxiii https://www.americafirstpolicy.com/issues/issue-brief-fatherlessness-and-its-effects-on-american-society#:~:text=18.3

xxiv https://mpaustin.org/the-extent-of-fatherlessness/#:~:text=24.7

xxv Section B, pg. 29, Fatherhood and Healthy Families Task Force of the President's Advisory Council report

xxvi Before the Personal Responsibility and Work Opportunity Act of 1996, the main welfare program was Aid to Families with Dependent Children (AFDC).

xxvii http://www.pewresearch.org/fact-tank/2015/06/18/5-facts-about-todays-fathers/

References

xxviii https://www.hopereflected.com/tag/do-everything-in-love

xxix Matthew 20:28

xxx 1 John 4:8

xxxi Luke 10:25-37

xxxii Promoting Responsible Fatherhood
http://fatherhood.hhs.gov/Parenting/index.shtml

xxxiii Numerous sources, including cultural organizations, educational institutions, and various articles on Maasai culture, confirm that the traditional Maasai greeting, "Kasserian ingera" (or variations like "Casserian Engeri" or "Eserian Nakera"), translates to "And how are the children?"

xxxiv Fatherhood Facts
http://www.dhr.state.al.us/page.asp?pageid=408

xxxv The Delinquents
http://www.cbsnews.com/stories/2000/08/22/60II/main226894.shtml

xxxvi http://www.todaysparent.com/blogs/run-at-home-mom/effects-of-moving-kids-mental-health/

xxxvii http://www.apa.org/news/press/releases/2010/06/moving-well-being.aspx

xxxviii "Children of mothers who change partners have higher rates of behavioural problems," *News - The University of Queensland*, February 12, 1998. (While this is a news article, it reports on specific research findings from the university).

[xxxix] Journal Issue: Marriage and Child Wellbeing Volume 15 Number 2 Fall 2005
http://futureofchildren.org/publications/journals/article/index.xml?journalid=37&articleid=107&sectionid=692

[xl] Matthew 5:9

[xli] 1 Cor 12:31

[xlii] Martin Luther King, Jr. (1929-1968). Stride Toward Freedom, 6, 1958

[xliii] Eph 4:26

[xliv] https://rtkendallministries.com/total-forgiveness-2

[xlv] Doing The Best I Can: Fatherhood In The Inner City. Katherine Edin & Timothy J. Nelson. University of California Press. www.ucpress.edu.

[xlvi] Fatherhood and Healthy Families Task Force of the President's Advisory Council

[xlvii] Psalm 68:5

[xlviii] Ephesians 6:4 King James Version

[xlix] http://www.fatherhood.org/mama-says-survey

[l] http://genius.com/Daniel-beaty-knock-knock-lyrics

[li] John 13:35

[lii] See Luke 10:27

[liii] 1 John 4:7-8

References

[liv] John 13:35

[lv] John 15:13

[lvi] *Bad Dads of the Bible: 8 Mistakes Every Dad Can Avoid* by Roland C. Warren—Zondervan

[lvii] http://warroomthemovie.com/about

[lviii] Genesis 3:1-13

[lix] Genesis 3:14-15

[lx] Revelation 20:1-3

[lxi] John 3:16-17

[lxii] Luke 15:11-32

[lxiii] 1 John 4:8

[lxiv] See Ps 34:17; Ps 91:11-12; Dan 6:22; Matt 18:10

[lxv] Galatians 6:7

[lxvi] Matt 11:28-30

[lxvii] Luke 19:10

[lxviii] The "I Have a Dream" speech is a monumental address delivered by Martin Luther King Jr. on August 28, 1963, during the March on Washington for Jobs and Freedom. It is widely considered one of the most significant and iconic speeches in American history.

lxix US Census Bureau Report
http://www.census.gov/prod/2008pubs/p70-114.pdf

lxx Learn about Urban Light Ministries at www.urbanlight.org

lxxi Learn about Nurturing Fathers Program at
http://nurturingfathers.com/

lxxii https://urbanlight.org/pops101/

lxxiii https://urbanlight.org/father-love/

lxxiv https://www.amazon.com/Fathering-Strong-Blueprint-Leading-Family/dp/B0F52HN91R

lxxv https://urbanlight.org/podcasts/

lxxvi https://urbanlight.org/latest-stories/

lxxvii https://www.fatheringstrong.com/

lxxviii https://www.prepinc.com/Content/CURRICULA/On-My-Shoulders.htm

lxxix http://www.fatherhood.org/

lxxx http://www.copes.org/clfc-fatherhood.php

lxxxi http://www.fatherhood.org/father-absence-statistics

lxxxii Tossed in a Sea of Change: A Status Update on the Responsible Fatherhood Field by Serena Klempin, MSW and Dr. Ronald B. Mincy

*Map and Track: State Initiatives to Encourage Responsible Fatherhood (Bernard & Knitzer, 1999).

References

---

lxxxiii Matthew 28:18-20

lxxxiv This phrase is attributed to Donald Rumsfeld, former US Secretary of Defense.

lxxxv Malachi 4:6

Notes

References

To learn more about Church-based Fatherhood Ministries or the additional resources that accompany this book please go to:

www.fatherlovebook.com

www.ingramcontent.com/pod-product-compliance
Lightning Source LLC
Chambersburg PA
CBHW030451100526
44580CB00005B/79/J